SELF-HYPNOSIS
KEY TO YOUR INNER POWER

GIL BOYNE

Edited by Dr. John Butler

SELF-HYPNOSIS: Key to your Inner Power
Copyright © 2017 by John Butler
Illustrations and cover design by Stuart McCrone –
copyright © 2017 by John Butler
All rights reserved. No part of this book may be reproduced or transmitted in any form or by any means without written permission from the copyright holder.

ISBN 978-0-9957097-2-0
Published by Westwood Publishing

With Gratitude for our Inner Power

CONTENTS

Introduction to Gil Boyne by Dr. John Butler 7

1 Hypnosis: Discover Your Inner Power 13

2 Release your Inner Power 19

3 Hypnosis + Suggestion = Programming 29

4 Imagination – for you or against you..................................37

5 The Hypnotic Contract 43

6 Self-Hypnosis – here it is 51

7 Increase your Hypnotic response 59

8 Putting a Hypnotic Session together 69

9 Getting your own Message – Rules of the Mind................81

10 Trance "Secrets" - 2 Routes, 5 Methods..........................97

11 A Full Programming Session - on Confidence...............107

12 Five Ways we gain Confidence in Ideas.........................115

13 Readiness for Change: 2 Steps, 3 Turning Points..........131

14 Programming: 4 Stages, 10 Rules...................................143

15 Hypnotizing & Programming Yourself: 153

Conclusion 171

Introduction to Gil Boyne

Gil Boyne, master hypnotist, therapist and trainer, believed passionately that change comes from within. He lived through a childhood in the 1920s in a tough neighborhood with a hard-drinking father, the Depression of the 1930s, the Second World War in which he saw active service as a teenager in the US Navy in the Pacific, the resurging prosperity of the 1950s, and the mind-expanding and revolutionary therapeutic movements of the 1960s, in which he was a very active participant.

He began working with hypnotherapy in the early 1950s, and in the 1970s and early 1980s drew together his ideas on therapy into a radical, advanced system, called Transforming Therapy™, which he carried on developing and refining until his passing in 2010. He studied with many great names of psychotherapy, psychiatry and hypnotherapy of the time and integrated the most valuable of their ideas into his own work.

He taught his self-hypnosis classes for over thirty years, to more than 20,000 students personally, in addition to many more who listened to his recordings worldwide. These recordings are available to accompany this book. His classes in Los Angeles attracted many celebrities, earning him the title "Therapist to the Stars" of stage and screen.

His fame as a therapist and trainer grew rapidly, making him one of the most influential and celebrated figures in contemporary hypnotherapy during the second half of the 20th Century. Schools of Transforming Therapy™, were set up with like-minded individuals to teach this extremely rapid, effective yet in-depth approach to hypnotherapy.

His students came to his self-hypnosis classes with a wide variety of personal goals, some of the most common being Relaxation,

Self-Confidence, Self-Discipline, Finding Life and Career Direction, Motivation, Health and Fitness including weight loss and smoking cessation, and overcoming performance nerves and creative blocks.

Gil believed that our inner world is concerned with our most basic physical needs, our complex emotional desires, and our highest spiritual aspirations, however perceived. His goal was to develop a method for people to fulfil their creative potential in the face of the many obstacles and opposing forces that life throws at us.

His teaching emphasizes the primary importance of gaining accurate and deep understanding, learning the ways the mind works, and developing the creative inner resources that he passionately believed to be the birthright of every human being. In his work he sought to restore awareness of this birthright to those he taught. The principles and techniques explained and described in this book are those he found the most reliable, powerful and valuable in achieving this goal, and he consistently taught these in his classes.

Gil's approach was in marked contrast to "techniques-based" systems of learning self-hypnosis. Although he possessed a dazzling skill in hypnotizing, and could draw on a vast repertoire of trance and programming methods, he never sought to pass on a "bag of tricks" to his students.

Instead, he taught them how to learn from every response, not to grasp blindly for a new "trick" whenever things do not "work", but to reach inside and see what their subconscious mind is conveying to them by responding as expected, or responding differently from expected, including no apparent response.

In this way, he sought to lead his students to gain confidence in their own inner powers, to reach out to the deeper layers of their own subconscious, and to start on a path to self-integration and deep inner harmony. On the way, many intermediate goals are achieved in a more sustainable, intelligent manner than by a fragmented, superficial approach.

This book consists of Gil's own words, drawn from his writings and from his recorded teachings on self-hypnosis. I have added only a small number of linking and clarifying sections based on my experience of studying his work in depth and working with him in his classes. The book does not focus on the numerous academic or very speculative theories of hypnosis, but on solid principles and powerful methods that provide practical and straightforward self-help for you.

Audio recordings of Gil's programming recordings are available from the Westwood Publishing website, along with further books of Gil's teachings, and films of him teaching and working with clients.

It is my sincere hope that his work continues to live in the changes his teaching brings to you.

Dr. John Butler
Director
Westwood Publishing
Hypnotherapy Training International

IMPORTANT NOTICE

Hypnosis and self-hypnosis are natural experiences of the mind and as such, are not hazardous in themselves. Many millions of people worldwide practice hypnosis and self-hypnosis to their great benefit, and research shows that its beneficial effects have much in common with those of meditation and similar practices.

Hypnosis and self-hypnosis are not recommended in this book as a substitute for medical or other treatments or diagnosis. They have many potential benefits working in harmony with any treatments that may be undertaken.

People with very traumatic personal histories, or severe emotional vulnerabilities, may find it best to seek expert support when first learning to practice hypnosis and self-hypnosis, however they can benefit from reading this book for information.

Caution and expert guidance are also strongly recommended in the case of epilepsy or psychosis, and in substance-induced altered states of consciousness. In these cases, it is recommended that a medical or other appropriate practitioner is consulted for guidance.

Hypnosis and self-hypnosis should NEVER be practiced when driving or doing any other activity that requires your conscious attention or control.

Chapter 1

HYPNOSIS – DISCOVER YOUR INNER POWER

You now stand on the threshold of a great adventure. You have used your power of decision in choosing to read this book. You have overcome the natural tendency to procrastinate, and you have decided to explore your potential for change. You have decided to take responsibility for bringing about positive and beneficial change in your life, and that's wonderful.

You are taking a step now that will enable you to mobilize your energy to work for you. You will begin to gain a new perception that will allow you to use your creative intelligence to change your life.

I want to teach you to enter hypnotic trance and to develop your trance ability. I want to teach you how to condition and program yourself so that your mental and emotional powers work for you. I don't use the term positive thinking, because I don't think it's possible to have only positive thoughts in your mind, and you don't need totally to override your natural self-protective instincts such as fear, in order to develop your creative potential. I want you instead to know that there are real obstacles, difficulties and people who will oppose you in the world, and this is never a reason to stop working towards your goals. I want to teach you to be a self-hypnotizer and a self-programmer, to take responsibility for yourself and to move into that exciting, new part of your existence called change.

Change because you direct it. Change because you decide you want it. Change because it's going to make your life happier, richer, more satisfying and more fulfilling.

Our purpose in this book is for you to learn the principles and methods that enable you to take control of your own energy. Then you can begin to channel it so that it works for you more of the time than it works against you. As you do that, you begin to move closer to a point in your personal development where the part of you that knows what is good, right, satisfying, rewarding, fulfilling and appropriate for you, agrees with what you feel like doing. In other words, a state of profound inner harmony that enables you to be a positive and balancing force in your environment.

How hypnosis works for you

Hypnosis makes the difference for many people in getting their own energy to work for them rather than against them. There are many methods that claim to bring about inner peace and release personal energy, and there are people who obtain results following these methods, but the special characteristics of hypnosis give a vital advantage in the struggle against external pressures, self-doubts and inner conflicts which hold many people back and limit their progress. I have studied, practiced and taught hypnosis for many decades. From my experiences with many thousands of clients and students, this is what I can tell you.

> **Hypnosis is first of all a natural state of mind, with special identifying characteristics. A capacity for response to hypnosis is a natural human ability.**
>
> **As hypnosis is a natural state of mind, there is nothing unnatural about hypnosis and there is nothing supernatural about it.**

The special characteristics of hypnosis, that give such a vital advantage to the individual in the struggle against external pressures, self-doubts and inner conflicts, are:

1. Hypnosis is a state that possesses an extraordinary quality of mental, physical and emotional relaxation.

Many people feel that for this quality of relaxation alone, it is worth learning self-hypnosis.

2. In hypnosis there is an emotionalized desire to satisfy the suggested behavior.

It is through this quality, of creating a desire to follow directions, that in self-hypnosis you gain the motivation to follow through on your plans.

3. Your body and mind move towards a balanced, self-regulating condition.

In hypnosis, your deep relaxation means that your body and mind are free to regulate themselves naturally, without the demands and stressors of the outside world.

4. Your sensory awareness – hearing, touch etc – can be heightened and selectively focused.

This is a very useful ability – you can decide for disturbing sensations or sounds not to bother you, for instance, or that your experience of pain or discomfort will be reduced, and focus on something else instead.

5. **Your habitual emotional and mental defensive responses are lessened.**

This is a very valuable quality for making changes in your life – you are more willing to consider expanding your horizons beyond old comfort zones and limitations.

Good news – no need to "Try"

In the next chapter, we're going to run through a few tests so that you can find out for yourself how your imagination responds to suggestion, and how powerful this can be. Now, because the word "test" for many people brings in the idea of effort, I'll explain here that trying has no place in responding to suggestion. There is a saying in this work, **"Trying is lying."** Someone might say, "I tried to feel it, to imagine it." Why is trying lying? *Because it implies the potential for failure, doesn't it?*

You don't have to *try*, because you can *do* it. Your imagination is capable of imagining anything that will be suggested in these tests, so there is no "trying" involved. If you set yourself to "try" to make it work, you are deciding in fact to resist, to counteract with one part of your mind what you are "trying" to do with the other, to doubt and argue with yourself. And that's not why you're here, is it?

Chapter 2

RELEASE YOUR INNER POWER

First we show, then we tell! I have a lot of information to give you about how you get the best out of your natural ability for hypnosis. But first, I want you to get excited about it, and the best way to do that is to test it for yourself.

If you were learning self-hypnosis in a client session or a class with me, obviously I would give you the instructions, however you can still easily perform these tests by one of the following:

1. Record yourself reading the instructions aloud.
2. Get someone else to read aloud and record the instructions,
3. Get someone else to read the instructions aloud to you in person.
4. Use some of my commercial recordings which are available for download from the Westwood Publishing website – westwoodpublishingco.com.

If you have a friend or colleague who is also interested in learning self-hypnosis, when you come to this section of the book, you can pair up and go through the exercises together, taking turns reading out the instructions.

> **Note: All of these exercises involve movements and actions which are common in everyday life. If you have any particular physical or other frailties which would make any of these actions inadvisable for you, omit or adapt as appropriate. Consult with your healthcare advisers if you require guidance.**

Test One: Heavy and Light Arms

<u>Posture:</u> Stand with your weight balanced evenly on your two feet. If you find it hard to stand, you can still do the exercise from a seated position. Extend both arms straight out in front of you. Reach out as far as you can. Leave your left hand facing down and with your right hand, turn the palm up so that it faces the ceiling. Curl the fingers of your right hand slightly.

<u>Preparation:</u> I'm going to start the directions by counting from three to one. As I count from three to one, first fix your gaze at a point on the wall or the ceiling, and as I reach the count of one, close your eyelids down. The moment that your eyelids close down, I want you to imagine that in your right hand I am placing a plastic pail. The handle of the pail will go right in the palm of your right hand. In that bucket there is wet sand which weighs about twenty pounds. As the bucket goes into your hand and you hold that picture in your imagination, you'll begin to feel the weight pulling your right hand down, down, down. Remember to keep your fingers curled, because if you uncurl them, the bucket might fall off.

At the same time that I put the bucket in your right hand, I'm going to tie a string around your left wrist. On the other end of that string is a large, three foot in diameter helium balloon. Since helium is lighter than air, when I release the balloon, it's going to tug your left hand right on up, higher and higher, as the right hand is being pulled down and down and down.

<u>Procedure (this part to be played/read aloud):</u> *Get ready now. Fix your gaze on a spot on the wall or the ceiling. Three, two, one. Close your eyelids down. Now I'm reaching out and I'm putting the bucket into your right hand. There it is. It's got twenty pounds of wet sand in it. You feel that weight. Be careful! Don't let it pull your hand*

down too quickly. On the other hand, don't struggle and try to force your arm up in order to show how strong you are.

Now I'm going to tie that string around your left wrist. Here I go, now! It's tied. On the other end of that string is that big helium-filled balloon. And it begins to draw your left hand right on up, higher, higher, coming up, moving up, as your right hand is being pulled down, down, down. What color is your pail? Become aware of the color of the pail. What color is your balloon as your left hand is being pulled higher, higher, higher and your right hand is being pulled down, down, down?

As you test your imagination, as you begin to become aware of your left arm rising higher, your right arm is being drawn down. Your right arm is being pulled down, and your left arm is going up and up and up. Higher and higher. Now I want you to stop. Don't move a muscle. Hold your arms exactly as they are and open your eyes. Look at where your arms are.

How did you do and what does it mean?

If your arms were very far or quite far apart, with your right arm down and your left arm up, you were responsive to this particular suggestion. By responding, you've demonstrated to yourself how powerful your imagination is, and how you can direct it to get the effects you want. Often, responsive people notice interesting things about the experience, such as how vivid the colors of the bucket and balloon were, how "real" and lively the experience felt, and even that their right arm was tired but their left arm was fine!

If your arms didn't move much, this is also something you can learn from. Think back carefully about what you were doing, in your mind. Often people who are reporting on their lack of responding will say things such as, "I was trying but I couldn't really feel it," "I felt you were making our arms tired by getting us to hold them out, and you were tricking us, so I resisted letting them move, I held them in place." These are all responses to learn from, to demonstrate to you that in this test, you chose to keep your conscious, critical ability active and analyze the experience, rather than letting your subconscious, imaginative ability respond spontaneously. This is the sort of initial reaction that people often have when learning to swim, for example, or ride a bicycle.

Keep practicing and you'll keep progressing.

Test Two: Arm Levitation

If you have a way to film yourself doing this test, this will be a useful learning tool for you. If not, don't worry, there are plenty of ways to learn!

Posture: Sit comfortably, placing both hands loosely on your thighs. Rest your two feet flat on the floor.

Preparation: In a moment, I will ask you to close your eyelids down. When your eyelids are closed, I will begin counting from one up to twenty. And as I count, I will suggest that a light, easy, pleasant feeling moves into your right hand and into your right arm. As I continue counting, that feeling grows stronger and stronger. Then soon you feel the first slight movement, slight movement of the fingers, a twitching of the muscles. Then your hand begins to lift. Your arm begins to lift and it continues moving, lifting and rising until it comes to rest over on your body.

Now when you feel that movement in your hand and in your arm as it's moving and lifting and rising and coming over to rest upon your body, don't try to resist. You *could* resist if you chose to, but that's not why you're here. I didn't say that this is an exercise to test your capacity for resistance. I said that these are exercises to test your capacity to respond!

Procedure (this section to be played/read aloud): *Get ready now. Three, two, one, close your eyelids down. I want you now to focus your attention down to your right hand. Without moving your fingers or your hand, become aware of the material in the garment beneath your fingertips.*

Now, I'm going to ask you to become even more aware, to increase your sensitivity. Explore with your mind what's going on in and around your right hand. For example, is your hand warm? Hot? Cool? Cold? Having made that decision, check it out in comparison to your left hand. Is your left hand's temperature different from that of your right hand?

Now with your mind go back to your right hand and check this. Is the palm of your right hand dry or moist? Go back and check the left hand. Is it the same as the right hand, or is it different? Now, over to the right hand once again. I want you to pick up the beating of the pulse in the wrist. Focus on that. Become very sensitive to it.

As I count from one up to twenty, that light, easy, pleasant feeling moves into your right hand and into your right arm. As I continue counting, that feeling grows stronger and stronger. Soon you'll feel the first slight movement, slight movements of the fingers, a twitching of the muscles. Then your hand begins to lift. Your arm begins to lift, and it continues moving, lifting, and rising until it comes to rest upon your chest or maybe on your chin or on your cheek or even on the top of your head.

When you feel that movement in your hand and in your arm, don't try to resist. You could resist if you chose to, but that's not why you're here. Just let your subconscious mind do its perfect work.

Number one. The first light, easy sensation moves into the fingertips of your right hand.
Number two. The feeling is spreading around beneath the fingernails.
On number three, it's moving up to the first joint of the fingers.
Number four, the first slight movement begins taking place; slight movements of the fingers, a twitching of the muscles.
Number five. That light sensation spreads across the back of your hand.
Number six. It's moving up and spreading up towards your wrist.
Now on number seven, at the same time, your left hand and arm begin to feel very heavy. Beginning to feel just as heavy as lead...
While on number eight the light sensation spreads through the palm of your right hand and it's beginning to move and to lift and to rise.
Now on number nine that light sensation has spread up and into your wrist.
Number ten. From the fingertips all the way up to the wrist your hand is light and free and beginning to lift. Just as light as a feather floating in the breeze and even lighter. As light as a gas-filled balloon. Just as a gas-filled balloon will rise and float toward the ceiling, in the same way that right hand is moving and lifting and rising.
Number eleven. Think of your left hand now. And your left hand feels as heavy as lead...
on number twelve your right hand is moving and lifting and rising.
Thirteen. It's spreading up toward your elbow now...
While on fourteen your hand is moving, lifting and rising and it may even go all of the way up to where it's pointing toward the ceiling.
On fifteen, into your elbow now. Your hand is so light and free that it's moving and lifting and rising. Coming up and moving up until it comes to rest upon your body. As you feel that movement, just let your hand continue to rise..
On sixteen, just rising and rising..
On number seventeen, moving and lifting and rising

On number eighteen, that's it. Let it continue. Moving, lifting and rising.
Number nineteen. That's good. On the next number now that hand is moving in toward your body..
Number twenty. Moving in until it touches your body.

<u>Termination and observation (this part to be played/read aloud):</u>
Now I'm going to count from three down to one, and as I count, your hands drop limply into your lap. Three, two, one. Let them drop limply, that's good. Now, I'm going to count from one up to three, and as I count, let your eyelids open, feeling fully awake and alert. One, two three. Let your eyelids open.

If you filmed yourself, look at the film. If someone was reading aloud and observing you, ask them what they saw.

How did you do and what does it mean?

Now I want you to know this, if you're concerned about a lack of response, **if you felt ANY sensation at all, you had 100% success.** Because what we're looking for is any change in response. If you take away the influence of suggestion in this test, then there's no logical reason why your hands and arms shouldn't have remained in your lap and continued to feel exactly as they did at the start. Therefore, if you felt any of the sensations mentioned, that's a change in response. Even if your hand never lifted off your leg at all, but if that hand felt lighter even though it didn't move up, that's a sensation and any sensation is one hundred percent response.

If your hand was moving ahead of the suggestions, so that it reached the resting point before the count of twenty, this shows you that your imagination, your subconscious mind, was able to start working itself from the description in the preparation section.

So you see that your subconscious mind is already picking up the skill of self-suggestion.

Conscious vs Subconscious responses

A question that often arises is "was I just making myself do it consciously, to conform or play along, or was there really a subconscious response?" So we will note here, the differences between conscious, voluntary movement and the subconscious type of responses that you've experienced in these suggestibility tests.

Conscious, Voluntary Movement

You can make a conscious decision now to raise your hand to your chest, and you can do it quickly or slowly. But when we make a movement consciously, there are always two characteristics present in that voluntary movement.

1. The movement takes place in a smooth, flowing motion. It is not a slow, jerky, erratic movement such as you saw happening in the suggestibility tests.

2. The movement is goal directed. In a conscious, voluntary movement, when you decide to move your hand to rest on your chest, your hand goes in a straight line from the starting place to where it is going to finish. It doesn't rise straight up, and then slowly swing over, and then down, and then in, to make contact with the body as we saw taking place in the Arm Levitation test.

Subconscious Response Movement

In a subconscious response, for instance in the Arm Levitation test, your hand moved in small increments and it moved in a number of directions, on its way to the goal. This tells you that you were experiencing a subconscious response. If you had been consciously directing it, it would have been smooth-flowing and would have traveled in a straight line from one point to another.

Spread it Around!

You may like to persuade a few of your friends to do these suggestibility tests, so that you can see for yourself the variety of responses they have. They have the same ideas presented to them, but their response is their own.

In that variety, and in that sameness, lies our suggestibility.

Chapter 3

HYPNOSIS + SUGGESTION = PROGRAMMING

The British psychiatrist, R.D. Laing, in his classic book, *The Politics of the Family*, has a chapter entitled, "Family Scenarios", in which he says, "The clinical hypnotherapist often knows what he is doing. The family hypnotist rarely does." What does he mean by that? Simply that the programming parents use with their children is in essence the same as we find being used in the clinical hypnosis setting.

In both situations, **we have the development of ideas that become emotionalized because of the nature of the ideas and their source.** We see those ideas becoming incorporated into what is called the "self image".

The clinical hypnotherapist uses hypnosis to bypass the **critical faculty** of the mind. The critical faculty (sometimes called the critical factor) is that aspect of the mind that evaluates and screens incoming ideas in terms of our previous experiences, our knowledge, and our past interpretations of our experiences. It is this critical faculty that the hypnotist bypasses in order successfully to present programming ideas to the subconscious mind.

But the parent talking to a young child doesn't need to bypass the critical faculty of the child's mind because the child has not yet developed a critical faculty. The critical faculty does not become effectively operational until about age eleven (when children often become critical of parents, much to the parents' dismay). Before we have a critical faculty with which to screen these incoming ideas, we accept them in the same way that we would accept ideas in hypnosis.

> Responses to suggestion take place because the critical faculty of the conscious mind that normally would process these ideas in terms of rationality is temporarily relaxed, but it hasn't disappeared.

I would like you to think of a stereo system. There is a control knob which is marked "balance". When you turn that knob all the way to the right, you hear the music only from the speaker through the right circuit. The speaker on the left becomes inactive. It doesn't disappear, but it's just not operational. When we turn the knob in the opposite way, to the left, then the right circuit becomes inoperative and the left circuit supplies all of the music.

In the same way, this critical faculty has temporarily been set aside so you can accept and act upon ideas without the need to evaluate them critically – without the need to say things like, "There's no reason for my right arm to rise," "There's no reason for my left arm to feel heavy." It is this that enables you to accept ideas about your own behavior that are different from your previous experience.

Our critical faculty is essential to us in our everyday life. But in self-hypnosis, we create a special state where we open ourselves to impressions. We use hypnosis to lower our psychic defenses and we use the suggestions that we have carefully selected, to achieve our truly desired goals. The time for analysis is over, and it is time for action.

Analysis inhibits responsiveness. You see, the critical faculty reasons with evaluation and analysis. The subconscious mind, on the other hand, reasons from effect back to cause. It is nonanalytic.

When we respond to suggestion, we have shifted into subconscious mode. When we don't respond, we are still clinging to our intellectual mode.

Suggestible or gullible?

Many people confuse "suggestion" and "suggestibility" with another concept, "gullibility". But "gullibility" means something entirely different. Gullibility means "the uncritical acceptance of ideas." The critical faculty of the conscious mind, which is the ability to critically examine incoming ideas through a filtering screen of past experience and interpretation, does not start to develop and become really effective until about age eleven. Prior to that time, we are very gullible. Actually, we are gullible all of our lives, but we are most gullible as young children.

Further on in this book, we will look at how our gullibility as young children can lead us to accept ideas about ourselves which are unhelpful and limiting, and how we can use self-hypnosis to change them. For now, I want you to understand clearly that suggestibility is desirable and helpful, while gullibility is not.

We can be suggestible and we can be gullible, but they are two different things.

Gullibility, being the uncritical acceptance of ideas, is a quality which puts us at risk.

Suggestibility, on the other hand, is a measure of the degree of intensity with which your brain and nervous system respond to incoming ideas. This is a desirable quality to have.

The best performers in sport, acting, music and other fields are the ones who are the most suggestible. If I use a different word, you will immediately understand it. The top performers are the most "**coachable**".

All top athletic performers, for instance, have been coached intensively along their path. They have had a series of coaches from when they started, usually as children, and they have repeated the moves they make in their sport thousands and thousands of times, with their coach paying intense attention and suggesting changes to their movements. The ones who succeed are the ones who can consistently respond to the suggestions their coach is making, improving their performance every day.

Not only performers need to be suggestible. All highly creative people are intensely suggestible. It means the ability to take an idea from outside yourself, bring it inside, create an image of it, and then express it as behavior, whether this is making a sculpture, writing a novel or coming up with a marketing campaign or a solution to a technical problem.

So the next time that someone uses the word "suggestible" in a demeaning manner, such as, "Oh, you're so suggestible," understand that it's great to be highly suggestible. Especially when you are suggestible in the ways that you want to be. It is true that highly suggestible people can be open to negative suggestion, often if they are particularly vulnerable because of their genetics and/or their personal history. It is especially important for people who are suggestible and highly sensitive or vulnerable to learn self-hypnosis, to ensure their suggestibility leads them in a positive direction and they enjoy a fuller, a freer and a happier life.

How Hypnosis by-passes the Critical Faculty

1: Hypnosis is a state that possesses an extraordinary quality of mental, physical and emotional relaxation.

I use the word "extraordinary" because this quality of relaxation at all levels does not occur in any other process. It does not occur in natural sleep, nor in drug use. There is no other way that you get that discharge of inappropriate, accumulated tensions from all levels of the organism. So the first characteristic is that it is an extraordinary quality of mental, physical and psychic relaxation that occurs *because you are hypnotized.*

2: In hypnosis there is an emotionalized desire to satisfy the suggested behavior.

When a person is hypnotized and carries out various suggestions that have been given to them, afterwards they may explain their behavior by saying, "Well, I did what you told me to do because I just felt like doing it." Or they explain that, "It was easier to do it than not to do it."

For example, suppose they were told that their eyelids were locked closed and then they were asked to try to open their eyes. When their eyelids don't open, afterwards they may explain their behavior by saying, "Well, I didn't open my eyes because I just didn't feel like opening them." Statements such as these are evidence of trance, because they indicate that an emotionalized desire to satisfy the suggested behavior is present.

The emotionalized desire to satisfy the suggested behavior comes about because of a factor called **rapport**. Trance helps to generate rapport, which is simply the subconscious relationship that develops between the person doing the hypnotizing and the person being hypnotized. Rapport is not what is called "transference", where in a course of therapy, the client has feelings about the therapist related to personal issues in the client's own therapeutic process.

> **Rapport is a genuine and valid relationship between two minds, chiefly at a subconscious level.**

Sigmund Freud said, "Hypnosis is a society of two." I say that it is a very delicate and very intimate relationship of two minds at a deeper level.

Although at first glance, this might not seem so relevant to self-hypnosis, often when we want to bring about change, we're having trouble with conflicting parts of ourselves – for instance, we are ambitious but this conflicts with our insecurities, or we want to be fit and healthy but this conflicts with our wish to indulge in comforting habits. So self-hypnosis is a way of getting into rapport with yourself, gaining self-awareness.

3: Heightened responsiveness to suggestion, direction and instruction

Notice that I didn't say, "An irresistible compulsion to obey the hypnotist and respond to that which is suggested." **Many people have a fictitious belief that no matter what the habit may be or how longstanding it is, all that is required in order to break it is to hypnotize the person and say, "Well, that's gone. You'll never do that anymore." But it's not that simple at all.**

Suggestions can be good or bad, voluntary or involuntary, conscious or subconscious.

> The complete definition of a suggestion is that it is "an idea that reaches the mind and stimulates action." *Until an idea reaches the mind and action is taken, it's not a suggestion.*

As an example, you can read a book that is full of ideas, but to fulfill the definition of a suggestion, those ideas must stimulate at least mental actions such as identification, interpretation, association, integration and so on.

Many hypnotists will state: "Hypnosis is the power of suggestion." But that's not true. Hypnosis is a natural state of mind, and we utilize suggestion with hypnosis, but they are not the same thing.

I like to use the word "programming" because it has the connotation of being something done deliberately and voluntarily.

> **Programming is something that we are fully aware of when we do it and it's taking place because we want it to.**
>
> **We have two different tools – hypnosis and suggestion – that we bring together to create effective programming.**

Chapter 4

IMAGINATION - FOR YOU OR AGAINST YOU

Can you recall, hopefully not too long ago, perhaps even this morning, awakening from sleep and feeling a sense of excitement? On those mornings, we feel hope, potential, what I call the "Challenge of Life", calling us to come out and to possess life in a fuller and richer measure than ever before. We're looking ahead, anticipating.

Sometimes we're able to look back upon what we've done in our life up to that moment. We're able to look at our performance and our achievement to date. We're able to measure who we are and what we have done against what we sense to be our potential.

To be able to look ahead at a potential future, to look back at our past and measure it against our present and our potential, is an amazing faculty. We can look across that great chasm called time from where we've been and where we are now, to that which we intuitively perceive we're capable of doing and being.

That faculty is our imagination.

The imagination can be a two-edged sword. It can work for us or against us, because

WHAT IS EXPECTED TENDS TO BE REALIZED

There are many factors which influence what occurs in our lives, but one of them is the expectations that fill our imaginations. In our efforts to make our life go the way we want, we often neglect this very powerful influence.

Self-hypnosis is the most effective way to use it for ourselves, rather than against ourselves.

We see this often in our own lives and the lives of those around us:

Those who fear rejection develop lifestyles and behaviors guaranteed to produce rejection from others, often becoming clinging and dependent, for example, or not developing a true character of their own because of seeking acceptance from others.

Those who have an intense fear of criticism develop lifestyles guaranteed to produce criticism from others, often becoming perfectionists, for example, or procrastinators.

Those who fear failure develop styles and approaches to life guaranteed to result in failure, for instance, through fear of risk failing to develop skills necessary for success, such as management of possibilities and change.

This is how we make sure our fears are realized – if we don't get rejected quickly enough, we become self-rejecting. If we aren't criticized often enough, we become intensely self-critical. If we don't fail through external circumstances often enough, we become self-saboteurs.

We undermine our own efforts.

What is expected has a powerful tendency to be realized, because

> **THE BRAIN AND NERVOUS SYSTEM RESPOND ONLY TO IMAGES**
>
> It doesn't matter whether those images are coming from outside of you through your perceptive senses or whether they are originating from within you through your faculty of imagination.

Dreaming

Dreaming is one kind of mental activity that involves the imagination. Take an example. If you're asleep in bed and you're having a nightmare, physically you are safe and comfortable. The doors and windows are locked, but your sleeping brain and nervous system doesn't know that. So your heart pounds at a rapid rate, you break out in a cold sweat, and perhaps the feelings of terror cause you to awaken. Even after you awake, the effects of the mental, emotional, and physical responses your imagination has created within you can be so powerful that it may be some time before you can even consider returning to sleep.

Daydreaming

Daydreaming is another imaginative mental activity. You can powerfully affect your nervous system by imagining, for instance, that you're off on a holiday, or playing with your favorite football team, or playing in a band. Whereas dreaming is always spontaneous, since it occurs while we are asleep, and daydreaming is often something we drift into without intending, we can daydream intentionally, perhaps to entertain ourselves while we're on a journey, or waiting for an appointment.

Memory

Memory also often involves the imagination, and can be spontaneous, as when good or bad memories are triggered by cues that set us off, such as an old tune or hearing someone's name, or deliberate, as when we set ourselves to remember, for instance, where we put something we now need to find.

Creativity

We also have the **deliberate creative use of the imagination.** Self-hypnosis and self-programming are some deliberate creative uses of the imagination. Problem-solving, invention and creative arts such as writing are some other creative uses.

So, next we're going to learn how to activate our natural faculty of hypnosis, and get our imagination to work for us, rather than against us.

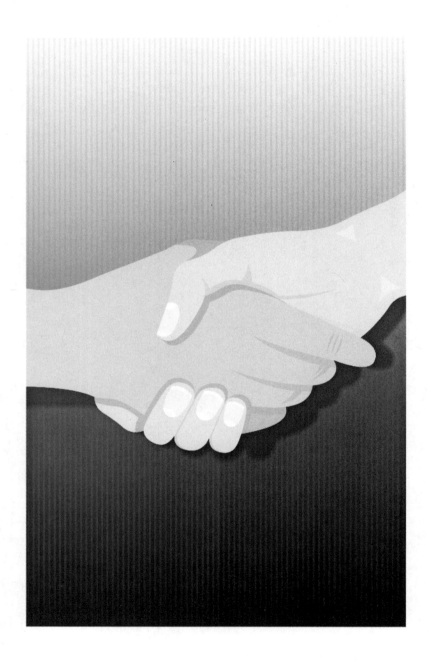

Chapter 5

THE HYPNOTIC CONTRACT

Hypnosis in an Instant

In my self-hypnosis classes, I give the following demonstration – there is a film of me doing it, which you can obtain and watch if you wish. I get people to line up in a row, standing closely one behind the other, and I tell them:

"I'm only going to do one thing. I'm going to shake your hand, and when I shake your hand you'll go into a trance right then. That's all it takes. When I come up to you, you will look at me, shake my hand, and in using this handshake technique you will go into a trance. You can stand in that trance. I'll take care of your balance. You needn't concern yourself with that. Do not fall to the floor. It is just too inconvenient to have bodies all over the floor! Now when you put your hand in mine, you look straight at me, stand and sleep."

Then I go up to the first student and say, "Put your hand in mine, now. Look at me." I then look intently into the student's eyes and at the same time tug sharply down with the hand they've just put in mine, and say in a sharp, commanding tone, "Stand and sleep!" As I say this, I bring my left hand up to cover their eyes, and bring their head down onto my chest, so I'm supporting the student. Then I say, "Stand; loosely, limply relaxed." As I say this, I prop the student back on their own feet, no longer leaning on me, and I shake the right hand that I tugged on, to loosen their right arm, and then let go of this hand, which will drop limply down to their side.

So the first student is hypnotized, in a few seconds. Then I shake the hand of the second student in the same way, but instead of bringing their head on my chest, I say, "I want you to put your hand in mine. Now look at me and... sleep [tugging their hand downwards]. Close your eyelids down. Head forward. [This brings their head to rest on the shoulders of the first student] Just rest and stand in perfect balance. Loosely, limply relaxed. That's good."

One after the other, I go through the line, until they are all hypnotized, standing in perfect balance, each one with their head on the shoulders of the one in front, and their arms hanging down loosely at their sides.

Rapid Deepening of Hypnotic Trance

Then I say to them all as a group, "Now, let every muscle and every nerve grow loose and limp and relaxed." And as I say this, I walk down the line of students, and one by one take each by the hand and shake their arm very lightly, then lift it a little bit up and let it fall down by their side again. Then I say, "Now you can continue going deeper with each easy breath that you take. That's the nature of your brain and nervous system. Just continue relaxing as you enjoy this trance."

Post-Hypnotic Suggestion for Rapid Reinduction of Trance

Then comes the really useful part – post-hypnotic suggestion, which means that I give a suggestion that will take effect after the trance session, when I give them a cue or trigger. I say to them, "For the remainder of this class, whenever I'm working with you, all that is necessary for me to do is to simply look at you, say two words, 'Sleep now', and snap my fingers [I demonstrate snapping my fingers so they can hear the sound clearly] and on the finger snap, your eyelids close down and you go deeply into hypnosis. Now, that takes place only in this room [safety suggestion]. Obviously, it wouldn't take place outside or if you're crossing the street, or in any circumstance in which you didn't have an environment of complete safety and comfort."

I then take them out of trance with a simple termination, and we have great fun as I chat to them, and at some point during the conversation, I say, "Sleep now!" and snap my fingers, and they instantly go into trance. I can also suggest to them that some other cue or trigger, such as when I touch the lobe of my right ear, will also act as a post-hypnotic suggestion. So I can be in a conversation with them, touch the lobe of my right ear casually, and they will again instantly fall into trance.

It's clear to everyone in the room, including the hypnotized person, that the extraordinary quality of mental, physical and emotional relaxation is present. The critical faculty of the mind has closed down to a great extent. It hasn't disappeared of course, it just steps aside while the trance is present, and as a result the hypnotized person can accept ideas and exhibit behavior that is different from the usual for that person. And this is what we want, the capacity for change!

So for the duration of the class, I'm then able to work with the students very rapidly, as inducing trance takes no time at all.

My classes are very lively! I use physical tests such as eye catalepsy and hand-locking, which we will come to later in this book, to bring them to an awareness that they are indeed in trance.

I usually demonstrate at least one completely "nonverbal" trance induction, such as bringing my hand down in a pass in front of a student's face. I explain that I'm demonstrating that there are many ways in which suggestions can be given and verbal suggestion is just one of a number of methods by which ideas can be conveyed to the mind in a manner that will result in a desired response.

Why do I put all this effort in?

Because I want them to understand where the true power of hypnosis is. There's no such thing as a hypnotic induction, in the sense of something that magically forces a person to go into a trance.

> **AN INDUCTION PROCEDURE IS NECESSARY, BUT THAT'S NOT WHAT INDUCES THE TRANCE.**
>
> **A HYPNOTIC INDUCTION IS A CONTRACT**

No matter what the form of the procedure, it is a way of my saying to the person, "I want you to go into a trance," **and they agree.** This is why trance can occur in an instant. Because this decision only takes an instant. Any time taken in an induction procedure, is leading up to that point, it's not the point itself. It's a process or ritual to get them there.

Why do they agree? That's the key question. Why do people say "Okay" within themselves and enter into trance when I indicate that I want them to go into a trance?

Trust

Because they trust me and they trust my competence to deal with them in trance because I have developed rapport with the group at this point. Instead of just talking about hypnosis, I'm up there doing it. That makes much more of an impression on the subconscious mind. When they watch me induce trance time and time again, they reach the point where they say, "He really can do what he said he would!"

They reason that I would only indicate that I can do certain things in hypnosis because I know absolutely, positively, beyond a shadow of a doubt, that I can do exactly what I tell them I'm going to do. And they're right! And they know that, whether they've thought about it consciously or not. That is called **mental expectancy** – that conclusion that they've come to, the decision that they've made, that I can and will do what I say I will. They **trust** me.

The whole purpose of what I do is to amaze them, that is, to cause them to open up to ideas they did not entertain before and to bring them to a certain realization, that every thing they're seeing demonstrated is a manifestation of a natural state of mind. And if it's a natural state of mind, that means that everyone can experience it, and if every one can experience it, so can you. I do it in such a way as to make it look mysterious, but it really isn't. I only choose to dramatize it in order to excite imagination and to develop mental expectancy.

Now, how does this apply to using self-hypnosis? The contract is just the same, only with yourself. Many people don't trust themselves, often with good reason! After all, they make contracts or bargains with themselves, and they don't keep them. They let themselves down. They say they will get fit, but they don't do anything about it; they say they will accomplish something, but they take no steps to do so. This means that you don't have a state of inner harmony, or self-trust.

So, achieving a powerful trance experience through self-hypnosis means starting to **trust yourself.**

The Trance Experience

I don't want you to have the misunderstanding that in hypnosis, people are zombie-like. Instead, you'll discover that it is as if for the first time you become aware of two levels of awareness. One part – the critical faculty – sits over here and laughs as it says, "Look at that going on! Isn't that the darndest thing you ever saw? Here I am with one arm up and one arm down, even though there's nothing there!" And another part of the mind is thinking, "Is that really right?" The critical faculty can step aside and smile in amusement, and the subconscious mind continues functioning.

This is most easily illustrated by an example. At the end of one of my professional hypnotherapy classes, the class asked me whether I would put on a demonstration of entertainment hypnosis, usually known as stage hypnosis. I agreed, and I told the class that they could invite friends, relatives and family members, especially those who had never been hypnotized, because we would use them in the demonstration.

On that night, I had twelve chairs in front of the room and asked for volunteers. As part of the show I created a mental illusion for them of an airplane trip and took them on a trip to Hawaii. All kinds of eventful things "happened" on the trip and they responded to the different events. After it was over, I invited each person to talk about their experience.

I walked up to the lady in the first chair and I said, "What was the most vivid, the most realistic part of that experience?" She replied, "Nothing. You said I was in an airplane, but I knew I was in a chair right in front of the room." I said, "Wasn't there anything in that experience that was in any way different from what you ordinarily experience while sitting in a chair in front of the room?" She thought about it for a minute and she said, "Well, I did start to feel nauseous." Then she paused for a moment before saying, "But there's nothing unusual about that. I get airsick every time I go on an airplane!"

That's a perfect example of the two levels of mind in operation. One part says, "I'm sitting in a chair in the front of the room," but the subconscious mind that's hearing the suggestions – "Now the plane is taking off and climbing" – is responding with the feeling that suddenly occurs in her stomach.

Hypnotism gives you that marvelous opportunity to discover what Dr. Freud said many years ago: "Yes, there are two levels of operation of mind." At one of those levels we have a reasonable degree of awareness, and at the other we have little conscious awareness. So, if trance depends on which level is dominant at any time, and they coexist at all times, **where is the line between trance and non-trance?**

It's a very thin line, and the important thing to realize is that because trance is a natural state of mind, it's okay to be in trance even when a hypnotist isn't working with you directly. You are in trance almost every day at one time or another, whether for a second or a minute or five minutes or ten minutes.

If you've ever become absorbed in a book or a movie, that's a form of trance behavior.

> **Trance behavior is when the critical faculty of the mind is set aside and another level of the mind is focusing and functioning easily and effortlessly.**

So now, let's experience it.

Chapter 6

SELF-HYPNOSIS – HERE IT IS

Get yourself into a comfortable position, ideally stretched out comfortably on your back, with pillows on the floor, or on your bed, or some other comfortable place. If you're not able to lie down, get into the most comfortable position that you can.

To listen to the directions, you can

1. Record yourself reading the instructions aloud.
2. Get someone else to read aloud and record the instructions.
3. Get someone else to read the instructions aloud to you in person.
4. Use some of my commercial recordings which are available for download from the Westwood Publishing website.

Play recording/read aloud:

You're about to enjoy a very pleasant and a very beneficial experience.

First, be sure that you will not be disturbed.
Second, remove your shoes or any apparel that will interfere with your comfort in any way.
Third, stretch out on your back with your legs separated so that no part of your calves or thighs are touching and separate your feet at least eight to ten inches, with your arms extended loosely and limply alongside your body, palms facing downward with your fingers limply outstretched.

Now, once we begin, you can help most by remaining quiet and passive.

Our first goal is for you to become unaware of your body. You can best achieve that goal by avoiding movement.

The first thing I want you to do is to fix your eyes on a spot on the wall or on the ceiling. Pick out a spot and stare at that spot without moving a muscle. Now, take a deep breath and fill up your lungs. Exhale slowly. Sleep now. Now a second and even deeper breath, take in all the air that your lungs can hold. Exhale slowly. Sleep now. And now a third deep breath, exhale. Sleep now.

Now let your eyelids close down. Your eyelids are closed down, please leave them closed down until I ask you to open them again. You'll always be able to open your eyes, unless I were to tell you that they're locked closed, and I don't intend to do that. You see, hypnosis is a state of mind, it is not a state of eyelids.

Now, I want you to picture and to imagine that you're looking at the muscles in the tips of the toes of your left foot. In your imagination, follow those muscles until they move back into the ball of the foot, back into the arch, and all the way back to the heel. Now turn all of those muscles loose. Let them grow limp and lazy, just like a handful of loose rubber bands.

Now, as the muscles begin to relax, just let your mind relax, too. Let your mind drift where it will. Let your mind drift off to pleasant scenes in your imagination. And now let the relaxation move on up, into the ankle now. From the ankle, all the way up to the left knee. The calf muscles begin to grow loose and limp and so relaxed. You're relaxing with each easy breath that you take. Begin breathing more deeply now, just as you breathe each night when you are deep and sound in slumber. Just imagine that you can see your breath as a white mist, coming from your nostrils. Each and every time that you exhale this white mist, you are freeing yourself of tensions, and going deeper, deeper into drowsy relaxation.

Now let the wave of relaxation that started in the toes of your left foot, just a few seconds ago, let it move over now into the toes of your right foot, and begin moving back, into the ball of the foot, back into the arch, and all the way back to the heel. Now turn all of those muscles loose, and go deeper in relaxation. Into the ankle, the muscles let go, and from the ankle, all the way up to the right knee. The calf muscles are turning loose and letting go.

You're relaxing more with each sound that you hear, each sound around you carries you deeper and sounder in sleep. From the knee, all the way up to the right hip, the long thigh muscles grow limp and lazy. Now, as those muscles relax, just go all the way down, deeper in drowsy slumber. Turn them all loose, and go deeper in slumber.

Now the wave of relaxation moves on up, into your stomach now, into the solar plexus, the center of nervous energy, each muscle and nerve lets loose, the tensions relaxing, you're drifting down, deeper and deeper in slumber. Up through the ribs, the muscles relax. Into the broad muscles of the chest, the muscles of the chest grow limp and loose and so relaxed.

All of your tensions are fading away. You're relaxing more with each easy beat of your heart, and going deeper in drowsy slumber. Into the neck, the muscles let go. All around the neck, the muscles relax, just as they relax each night, when you are deep and sound in slumber.

Now let the relaxation start down your back, from the base of the skull to the base of the spine, each muscle and nerve along the spine lets loose, relaxing. You're drifting down, deeper in drowsy slumber. Let the wave of relaxation spread out, into the broad muscles of the back, and all across the small of the back, all across the back of the shoulders. Turn loose every muscle and every nerve in the back, and go deeper in drowsy slumber.

Into the shoulders the muscles let go, from the shoulders down to the elbows, of both arms, the upper arm muscles are turning loose, easing off and just relaxing now. From the elbows down to the wrists of both arms, the forearm muscles grow limp and lazy. From the wrist to the fingertips of both hands, each muscle and nerve lets loose, the tensions relaxing, you're drifting down, deeper in drowsy slumber.

Into the jaws, the muscles relax. The jaws are parting slightly, teeth not quite touching, all around the mouth, the muscles smoothly let go. Up through the nose, each nerve gives way. All around the eyes, the muscles are heavy and so relaxed. Even your eyebrows are relaxing now. Across the forehead, the muscles smooth out. Across the top of the scalp, down the back of the neck, down through the temples and back around the ears, all of the muscles are loose and lazy, just like a handful of loose rubber bands.

And you may feel now that pleasant tingling sensation in the tips of your toes or in your fingertips or in other parts of your body. A pleasant tingling sensation growing stronger and stronger now as your entire body is being bathed in the pleasant glow of complete and utter relaxation. Now you are completely relaxed. Each muscle and nerve in your body is loose and limp and relaxed, and you feel good.

And as you go deeper into relaxation, you're becoming aware of just how much you really do enjoy slumber. You look forward to sleeping easily. You anticipate quiet and restful slumber, which is so beneficial and so rewarding. Sleep is your friend, of both your mind and your body, and it helps you and it heals you. You are totally enveloped in the soothing and gentle repose of deep sleep.

Every living creature has a dormant period each day. Even flowers sleep at night, for sleep is nature's great restorer. Sleep "knits up the raveled sleeve of care". You sleep like a log, soundly and deeply. Sleep bathes your entire being in total relaxation. A peaceful calm engulfs you and cradles you. You are suspended on a heavenly cushion of soft tranquility. You are so calm and peaceful, so much at ease. The velvet comfort of sleep is pleasing, it delights you.

You feel free. You feel rested. Your mind and your body respond easily and happily to the gentle languor of sleep. You're invigorated, revitalized and rejuvenated by natural slumber. You sleep deeply, soundly and continuously, all night long. You thoroughly enjoy the restoring power of natural slumber. You slumber quietly and peacefully, knowing that infinite life with its abundant goodness continuously operates through your thoughts and out into your every activity, for you feel good. Deep slumber makes you feel great. You waken each day, feeling alive and ready to begin a wonderful new day.

Each of these ideas is making a vivid, deep and permanent impression on your subconscious mind, and from this time forward with each passing day, you become more aware of a wonderful feeling of personal confidence. Confidence, as you realize that each day brings you one step closer to your goal. So that you now begin to enjoy a fuller and a more expressive life.

Now I'm going to slowly count from one to five, and then I'm going to say "fully aware". At the count of five, let your eyelids open, and you are then calm, rested, refreshed, relaxed, fully aware, feeling good in every way.

One, slowly, calmly, easily and gently, returning to your full awareness once again.
Two, each muscle and nerve in your body is loose and limp and relaxed and you feel wonderfully good.
Three, from head to toe you're feeling perfect in every way.
On number four, your eyes begin to feel sparkling clear, just as though they were bathed in cold spring water.
On the next number now, let your eyelids open, and you are then calm, rested, fully aware, feeling good in every way — number five,

eyelids open now, you are fully aware, take a deep breath, fill up your lungs, and stretch.

How did you do?

If you experienced anything at all, other than the sensation of lying down, you had 100% success! Because other than your response to hypnotic suggestion, there was no reason for you to feel anything else. So you responded, and that's wonderful. You're on your way.

As part of the intense relaxation of the brain and nervous system in hypnosis, people sometimes report sensations that occur spontaneously. All of these are natural and welcome signs of the shift into deep relaxation, enjoy them! They may include

- the sensation of feeling very heavy, as if you are sinking down into the floor
- the sensation of being very light – even to feeling as if your body were floating above the floor
- the feeling that one or both of your arms have raised in the air and your hands have turned over
- becoming unaware of your hands, your arms, your feet and legs, or perhaps even unaware of your entire body
- a sensation of swaying, or swinging as in a hammock
- sudden jerks of parts of your body as stored tensions are released
- the sensation that your body is seeming to expand like a large vinyl balloon blowing up or shrinking like that same balloon with the air being expelled
- the feeling that it took a long time
- the feeling that it took a very short time

You might experience all of those sensations, one or two of them or none of them, or other sensations. This is your individual response.

I'll also mention here the matter of snoring, as sometimes people are confused that while in trance, they may become aware that they are snoring. Trance is not sleep, but in both trance and sleep, two things occur which together result in snoring: one is deep, involuntary breathing, the other is a degree of relaxation occurring in the throat, palate and nose which results in relaxation of the breathing apparatus, and when you're lying on your back, can result in snoring.

Did you enter into a hypnotic contract? Did you experience trance?

Most probably, you did, or you moved closer toward it. Later on, we'll practice this again, and we'll use some methods to check whether you experience trance or not. Don't worry that you remained aware the whole time.

> **Trance is not unconsciousness. Your conscious awareness can drift away, but you don't become unconscious, and you can, if you wish, remain aware of everything that is going on.**

Chapter 7

INCREASE YOUR HYPNOTIC RESPONSE

Some people respond with greater ease or speed to hypnosis than others. How or why is this?

The difference is in a factor called *"inhibition on response"*. This has sometimes been called "resistance". You hear some hypnotists say, "Some people are resistant to hypnosis". This term has typically been applied to people who do not immediately respond with a high degree of responsiveness. When the expected response is not forthcoming, certain hypnotists will say, "You're resisting".

I don't believe this is the correct way to approach the situation. As the client, you've gone to the trouble to be there, you've paid your money, and now someone tells you that you're resisting! Then, when you say that you're not resisting, the hypnotist goes on to say, "I don't mean that you're resisting consciously, but you're resisting *unconsciously.*"

All this statement does is lead a client to feel that they can never be hypnotized because there are unknown forces at work outside their conscious awareness that prevent them from responding to hypnosis. So I don't recommend using the word "resistance", because it simply doesn't apply. Instead, we bypass that and we call it an inhibition on response. Everyone accepts the fact that we have inhibitions of various kinds.

In my experience, inhibitions on this natural state of mind that we call hypnosis develop from two main sources, misinformation and fear.

Misinformation about hypnosis

From the time you were very young until very recently, it's quite likely that all the information that you got about the subject of hypnosis was misinformation. When you were growing up, if someone came under the influence of other people, and started acting differently from how they had before, in a way that met with disapproval from others, you might have heard people say, "Oh, that new best friend of hers has her hypnotized, she does everything her friend does", or "That woman has him hypnotized into spending all his money on her." As you struggled to attach a meaning to a word that was new to you at that time, the meaning emerged: "If it's a mysterious influence that can't be explained, then call it hypnotism."

Even the media, which is supposed to be oriented toward factual reporting, promotes misinformation along these same lines. I recall the time of the infamous Charles Manson Family, where a small group of young people under the leadership of Charles Manson, a former convict and would-be revolutionary, committed a number of brutal murders in the Los Angeles area. When he was apprehended, the newspapers said, "Manson Hypnotizes Family Members!"

I called a newspaper and was referred to the police official in charge of public relations and press releases. I asked him, "What does it mean that Charles Manson hypnotized the family members? Did some hypnotism school director like me say, 'Yes, he was a student. I trained him to hypnotize'?" The official said, "No." I said, "Perhaps when you arrested him you found a collection of hypnosis books on the shelf that indicated that he might have been self-taught?" He replied, "No, that wasn't it." I said, "Well then, perhaps someone said to you, 'He hypnotized these people. I saw him do it.'" He said, "No, that wasn't it at all." I said, "Can you explain your use of the term?" He answered,

"Well, everyone knows what that means. He exerted a powerful influence over them. The proof is that they committed these murders at his command."

That is not a definition of hypnosis: "One who responds to a powerful influence."

The Manson Family have all now been incarcerated for many years and a book has been written about the case by the prosecuting attorney. It was evident that there were many factors leading to the influence Manson exercised over his followers. He was a very charismatic individual. In the environment he created and in the circles in which he moved, he gave a message of great intensity. Since like attracts like, he attracted a certain number of followers. He provided them with settings for drug abuse and sex orgies, and that was an influence, but hypnosis was never a part of it. Yet you see how misunderstanding can develop.

There are many ways to influence people, which do not involve hypnosis, a principal one being to supply them with false or partial information, and prevent them from accessing other information. Yet, the idea that hypnosis must be involved if a powerful influence occurs, still has a hold in the imagination of the public. Even popular songs perpetuate the myths. In talking about falling in love, the lyrics say, "Those eyes hypnotized me." What they're saying is, "This mysterious process which generates such strange feelings within me and produces behavior I don't even fully understand must mean that I'm hypnotized." Again, a faulty interpretation and incorrect labeling!

How do we overcome misunderstanding? Misunderstanding is overcome through **reeducation**. The acceptance of the original ideas is the education. The altering, amending or replacing of these ideas is reeducation. We'll discuss this further later in the book, when we come to learn about how ideas are accepted in the mind.

Fears about hypnosis

A second way that inhibition on response develops is because of subconscious fears. The idea of hypnosis often brings up fears in people, primarily a fear of loss of control. When you think about the fact that the worldwide sales of anti-anxiety medications run into billions each year, you begin to recognize that there are a lot of people who feel that they are losing control or are out of control. Many people view hypnosis as an element that could reduce or remove their control if they allowed themselves to be responsive to hypnotic induction.

- Sometimes the fear may take the form of being controlled by another – the hypnotist.

- Sometimes people fear that they will reveal all their secrets when they're hypnotized.

- Sometimes people fear that those parts of themselves that make them uncomfortable and which they don't allow to emerge very often might be released in hypnosis. "If I ever really let go, what would happen?", "If I ever really felt all of my sexual feelings, what would happen?", "If I ever really felt all of my sad feelings, what would happen?" So the fear is that hypnosis might break down or remove all of the controls so that all of this energy just emerges. Sometimes this fear takes the form that there is a whole hidden "secret self" which may emerge, like Dr. Jekyll and Mr. Hyde.

- Sometimes people fear that they will be "stuck" in hypnosis, unable to return to their usual state of consciousness.

If any of these common fears is present, responsiveness to hypnosis can be inhibited as a result.

The ideas upon which these fears are based are mostly false. They come from dramatic motion pictures, cartoons and comic strips that in general contain ideas about hypnosis that are nothing more than figments of a screenwriter's imagination. The hypnotist does not have power to make you do anything without your consent. Without your consent, you will not reveal things about yourself that you don't want to. Without your consent, parts of yourself that are in your control will not become out of your control. And there is no known case of anyone being permanently "stuck" in hypnosis – there are rare times when people do not come out of hypnosis immediately on command, but this is usually because they don't want to, and if left alone, they will come out spontaneously when they are ready.

However, there is a kind of basis for some of these ideas, in that the trance is a powerful state that does automatically soften psychic defenses. That's one reason it is a very rapid therapy. In the traditional talk therapies it could take weeks of talk to get to some important subconscious energies, ideas or elements. In hypnotherapy, because of this automatic softening of defenses, you can move to that place much more quickly. And there's something very important to realize:

> **Hypnotic response is not a process in which you lose control – it is a process in which you GAIN control.**

How do you gain control? Usually, your subconscious fears and desires are hidden, or partly hidden, from your conscious attention. Through hypnosis, you can become much more aware of them, and integrate the power of your subconscious energy with your conscious goals. And you enter into hypnosis, from the outset, with consent and awareness.

Transforming nervousness

Let's demonstrate how that control can be exercised, by taking a simple way of transforming a subconscious fear of hypnosis. You may sense that you hold back, you're inhibiting your response. You might say you're nervous. Instead of using the word "nervous", let's use a more accurate word that will enable you to assume greater control over what you are experiencing. Let's change the word to "excited". Say, "I'm excited." You're feeling an excitement in your nervous system. But when you go to describe what you're experiencing, if you say, "I'm nervous", that sounds kind of negative and makes you feel bad, doesn't it? On the other hand, if you say, "I'm excited", that sounds very positive and makes you feel good. Yet the feeling that you're describing is the same thing. When you learn to program yourself, you take control through these types of transformations.

Practice makes progress

For many people, the word "discipline" rings the wrong kind of bell. When they think of discipline they think of punishments and restrictions being enforced on them as a child. But discipline really means a **willingness to pay the price**. And a willingness to pay the price really means taking control, taking *full* responsibility for your life.

This is very important because if in any area of your life you cling to feelings of helplessness, you learn to develop a secondary payoff. You begin to engage in behavior calculated to get sympathy or to get attention or designed to punish yourself or to punish others, in order to avoid the responsibility of doing and being and succeeding.

In that payoff, you give up your true aspirations and become shut off from your inner creative intelligence that can take a problem or an obstacle, address itself with full commitment, and learn what to do to overcome it and how to do it.

So the question always is, what do *I* do to achieve my goals? *Not* what someone else should do or should have done.

Discipline = Willingness to do what it takes

No matter how talented you may be, there is still a great deal to be said for having the self-discipline to pay the price that ensures success in life. There are many well-known sayings that reflect this, such as Thomas Edison's statement that "Genius is one percent inspiration, and ninety-nine percent perspiration."

Your strength in self-hypnosis builds with every time you practice it.

This reflects the fact that habits of thinking, and habits of behaving, are created and strengthened over many repetitions, often that take place over a long period of time.

It's all fun!

Fortunately, it's very pleasant work! Approached with optimism and enthusiasm, practice is something you look forward to. Remember that Edison also said he had never done a day's "work" in his life, because he was enthusiastic about what he did, "it was all fun."

> **Each time you practice self-hypnosis, listening regularly to the inductions and suggestions, you make it easier and stronger the next time. And you don't have to force yourself to concentrate, to pay attention or to listen, because the less your conscious effort, the more your subconscious response.**

The most powerful way to practice is to do it every day at the same time and in the same place. Get as near to this as you can – if the same place isn't possible, then practice at the same time, or use a small range of times and places. Use the scripts and recordings that we've already done, and add the new ones in to your practice as we encounter them in later chapters. Start today, not tomorrow.

Remember that "trying" is lying!

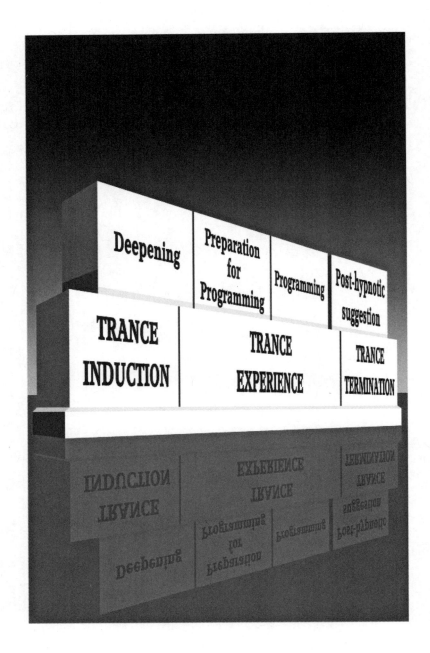

Chapter 8

PUTTING A HYPNOTIC SESSION TOGETHER

A hypnotic session has a routine, a structure, just like a physical exercise session has a routine. In a physical exercise session, the basics are
- warm-up
- training
- cool-down

because this suits the nature of your muscles. The three basics of a hypnotic session are
- trance induction – in this stage, the trance is "created", that is, you take the decision to enter trance, setting the critical faculty temporarily aside
- trance experience – you then have a period of time in this special state, which you can use in different ways
- trance termination – you choose to exit the trance, setting your critical faculty back into action once again

because this suits the nature of your mind.

The "trance experience" can be "neutral trance", where you are simply aware of the experience of your body relaxing. This is a very valuable "resting" experience in itself. The "trance experience" section is also your opportunity to add in some of the most common ways of using trance, for instance,
- deepeners
- suggestibility testing
- programming
- post-hypnotic suggestion.

To demonstrate, now we'll practice another trance session, adding in deepening, suggestibility testing, post-hypnotic suggestion, and programming. You'll see that the structure can be quite flexible, and suggestibility testing, for instance, can often have a deepening effect, i.e. you are usually more completely in trance after a suggestibility test than when you started it, so there is overlap between these methods.

This time the trance induction will be similar, but not exactly the same, as the one you had before. It's a little speeded up as you're progressing now in your practice. And we're going to do one suggestibility test that you did before, to see how it goes when you're in trance, and then two new tests as well. You may wish to film yourself, so that you can see how you respond to these tests.

As well as trance and testing, we're going to do a very brief programming so that you can get started on this, and make good use of the trance you achieve.

Preparation

Get yourself comfortable lying down with pillows on the floor, or lying on your bed or couch. If you are not able to lie down, sit back comfortably. This time, the sections of the routine – induction, deepening, trance etc - are noted on the script below, so you can get used to how a trance and programming session is put together, preparing for when you're putting sessions together for yourself.

If you had some inhibition on response the first time we did the arm levitation test, you can use the version of the script with additional "arm-pulling" to give you an extra lift this time.

You've stretched out comfortably on your back with your legs separated so that no part of your calves or thighs are touching. Fix your eyes on a spot on the ceiling overhead. Pick out an imaginary spot and stare at that spot without moving a muscle. If there is light in your eyes at this moment, you can close your eyelids down. If not, you can just keep staring at that spot.

Play recording/read aloud

Induction: Take a deep breath now and fill up your lungs. Exhale slowly. Sleep now. Now a second and even deeper breath. Exhale. Sleep now. Now let your eyelids close down as a wave of heavy relaxation begins to move all across your body and each muscle and nerve begins to grow loose and limp and lazy. Each time that you relax like this, you relax more fully, more quickly and more easily. Hypnotic relaxation is a skill that you are easily developing with your practice.

Now let the wave of relaxation move into the toes of both feet and quickly move back into the arches – all the way back to the heels. And now turn all of those muscles loose. Let them grow limp and lazy, just like a handful of loose rubber bands.

Now, as the muscles begin to relax, just let your mind relax, too. Let your mind drift where it will – to pleasant scenes in your imagination. As into the ankles the muscles let go – from the ankle all the way up to the knees of both legs. The calf muscles grow loose and limp and so relaxed. You're relaxing with each easy beat of your heart and going deeper, deeper in drowsy slumber.

From the knees all the way up to the hips of both legs, the long thigh muscles are turning loose and letting go. Now, as those muscles relax, just let go a little more. Gently, calmly, easily drift on over into a pleasant state of relaxation. Into the stomach, the muscles let go. Into the solar plexus, the center of nervous energy, each muscle and nerve lets loose, relaxing. You're drifting down, deeper and deeper in sleep.

Up through the ribs, the muscles let go. Into the broad muscles of the chest, the muscles of the chest grow loose and limp and so relaxed.

You're relaxing more with each easy breath that you take. You're breathing more deeply now, just as you breathe each night when you are deep and sound in slumber. Into the neck, the muscles relax. As the relaxation starts down your back, from the base of the skull to the base of the spine, each muscle and nerve along the spine lets loose, relaxing. You're drifting down, deeper and deeper in sleep.

Into the shoulders, the muscles let go, from the shoulders down to the elbows, from the elbows down to the wrists. The forearm muscles are turning loose and just relaxing now. From the wrists to the fingertips of both hands, each muscle and nerve lets loose, relaxing. You're drifting down, deeper and deeper in sleep.

Into the jaws, the muscles relax. The jaws are parting slightly – teeth not quite touching – all around the mouth, the muscles smoothly relax. Up through the nose, each nerve gives way. All around the eyes, the muscles are heavy and so relaxed. Even your eyebrows are relaxing now. Across the forehead, the muscles smooth out. Across the top of the scalp, down the back of the neck and down through the temples and back around the ears, all of the muscles are loose and lazy.

<u>*Deepener (this deepener uses awareness of your own physical sensations to deepen your trance):*</u> *You may feel now that pleasant tingling sensation in the tips of your toes or in your fingertips or in other parts of your body. A pleasant tingling sensation growing stronger and stronger now as your entire body is being bathed in the pleasant glow of complete and utter relaxation. Now you are completely relaxed.*

<u>*Post-hypnotic suggestion:*</u> *Each time that you relax like this, you relax more quickly, fully and more easily.*

Suggestibility tests (suggestibility tests in trance have the effect of Deepening the trance): *This time I am going to count from one up to twenty, and as I do, that light, pleasant feeling moves into your right hand and into your right arm. As I continue counting, that feeling grows stronger and stronger and soon you'll feel the first slight movements, a twitching of the fingers and then your hand begins to lift. Your arm begins to lift, and it continues moving, lifting, and rising until it comes to rest upon your chest or maybe on your chin or on your cheek or even on the top of your head.*

When you feel the movement in your hand and in your arm, don't try to resist. You could resist if you chose to, but that's not why you're here. Just let your subconscious mind do its perfect work. Now, we're ready to begin.

Number one. The first light, easy sensation moves into the fingertips of your right hand.
Number two. The feeling is spreading around beneath the fingernails.
Number three, it's moving up to the first joint of the fingers.
Number four, spreading to the large knuckles across the back of the hand.
Number five, the first slight movements begin taking place, slight movements of the fingers, a twitching of the muscles.
Number six, that light sensation continues to move.
Number seven, your right hand growing lighter and lighter with each number I count.
While on number eight, your left hand and arm begin to feel very heavy, just as though they were made of lead or marble or stone.
Number nine, that light sensation spreads through your wrist, through the palm of your hand, across the palm of your hand through your thumb, and your hand begins moving and lifting and rising.
Number ten, from the fingertips all the way up to the wrist, your hand is light and free and lifting, just as light as a feather floating in the breeze and even lighter, as light as a gas-filled balloon. Just as

that gas-filled balloon will rise and float toward the ceiling, your right hand is now moving and lifting and rising.
Number eleven. It's beyond the wrist and moving into the forearm now., coming up and moving now. Moving, lifting and rising, moving and lifting and rising, until it comes right up upon your body.
Number twelve, think of your left hand again. Your left hand feels heavy, as though it were made of marble, stone or lead and far too heavy to lift.
While on thirteen, the right hand now is moving and lifting and rising and coming right on up, until it comes to rest up upon your body.
Fourteen, it's moving up and into your elbow. From the fingertips all the way up to your elbow, your hand is light and free and lifting, just as light as a feather floating in the breeze and even lighter. As light as a gas-filled balloon.
Fifteen. Just as that gas-filled balloon will rise and float towards the ceiling, your right hand is moving up and when it comes to rest upon your body, your eyelids lock so tightly closed, that the more you try to open them, the tighter they're locking closed.
Sixteen. Beyond the elbow, moving into the upper arm.
Seventeen, moving and lifting and rising.
Number eighteen, when your hand touches your body, at that point your eyelids lock so tightly closed, that the more you try to open them, the tighter they're locking closed.
Number nineteen, on the next number now, your hand is light and free and coming up to the position where it's going to rest.
Number twenty, now your hand is moving in and when it comes to rest upon your body you find your left arm feels so heavy and your eyelids lock so tightly closed, the more you try to open your eyelids, once your hand has touched your body, the more you find them locking closed.

[Extra suggestions for more inhibited responders:

I want you to imagine there's a pulley in the ceiling. It is a red plastic pulley, and a blue rope that runs up through the pulley and *then down again. I'm going to count three numbers and tie the rope around your wrist. I'll pull down on my end, and as I do, I pull your hand right on up.*

One. Tying one end of that blue rope right around your wrist.
Two. Grasping my end and pulling down.
And three – as I do, it draws your hand right on up.

Good, right on up and coming up, I reach up and take it again and pull it right on up and here it comes. That's it. And right on over on your body. I'm reaching up once more and pulling it, pulling it, pulling it, and it's drawing your hand right on up until it comes to rest over on your body. That's it. Now I pull one more time. It comes to rest on your body and as it does, your eyelids have locked so tightly closed, the more you try to open them, the tighter they're locking closed.]

Make a try and satisfy your self that your eyelids have indeed locked tightly closed [3-second pause].

Alright, stop trying and just relax because at this time, your left arm feels as though it were made of marble. Your left arm feels so heavy that just the thought of lifting it is more than you want to deal with at this time. You may, if you wish, make an effort to lift that left arm, but it just feels as though it were made of marble or stone or lead and the thought of trying to lift your left arm is more than you want to deal with. However, if you wish, you make an effort to lift the left arm, but it's just too heavy to lift.

Now, I'm going to count to three and your left arm will feel normal, the same as your right arm. One, two, three and the heaviness instantly leaves your left arm and feels normal.

I want you now to raise both arms when I count to three. Raise them deliberately and point them straight up towards the ceiling in a straight line from your fingertips all the way back to your shoulders.

Alright, one, get ready to raise both of your arms. Two, begin lifting them now, do it now. Three, point both of your arms straight up towards the ceiling. Turn your hands so the palms of your hands are facing each other, your arms extended in a straight line from your shoulders to your fingertips. As I count to three, bring the palms of your hands together. One, two, three. Bring the palms of your hands together and now interlock your fingers. Interlock your fingers. Stiffen your arms. Lock your elbows. Squeeze your fingers very tightly against the backs of your hands. Even tighter. Imagine your two hands are carved of one solid block of wood. Locked so tightly closed, the more you try to pull your hands apart, the tighter they're locking closed.

Try now to pull your hands apart and find them locking tighter and tighter. Make the try and satisfy yourself and you'll see they are indeed locked tightly closed. Even though you try to pull them apart, they just remain stuck.

Now I'm going to count from three down to one, and when I do, your fingers relax, you can pull your hands apart, and they drop instantly down, limply to your side – all at the same time. Get ready now, three, fingers loosening, two, begin drawing them apart, one, drop them limply to your side and go much deeper into hypnosis.

<u>*Preparation for Programming:*</u> *The feeling that you felt as your right arm was lifting, that's the feeling of hypnosis. The feeling that you felt as your left arm seemed so heavy, that too is the feeling of hypnosis. Responses to suggestion take place because the critical factor or faculty of the conscious mind that normally would process these ideas in terms of rationality is temporarily relaxed, but it hasn't disappeared. This critical factor has temporarily been set aside so you can accept and act upon ideas without the need to evaluate them critically. It is this single faculty that enables you to accept ideas about your own behavior that is different from your previous experience.*

Programming: Things that you found difficult to do will now be easy to do, for you are a unique and extraordinary individual. There are things for you to do that can and should be done better by you than by any other person. Never before has life been expressed by any other person in exactly the way it is now being expressed by you. If it had been, there wouldn't be a reason for you to be here. Never again on this planet will life be expressed in the same way it is now being expressed through you. For if that were part of the plan, there'd be no need for you to be here now.

You accept yourself as a lovable person. You easily express love and affection and approval and you eagerly accept the love and approval that surrounds you now.

Post-Hypnotic Suggestion: You'll find that each time you use this method for easy relaxation, you relax more quickly and more easily and more fully. And as you do, your subconscious mind becomes even more accessible. You see, it's the nature of your subconscious mind to respond to ideas that it perceives are based in truth and in reality. So be it. Not because I've said so, but because that's the nature of your mind.

Trance Termination: I'm going to count from one to five and then I'm going to say, "Fully aware". At the count of five, please let your eyelids open. You are calm, rested, refreshed and relaxed and you feel wonderfully good in every way.

One. Slowly, calmly, easily and gently returning to your full awareness once again.
Two. Each muscle and nerve in your body is loose and limp and relaxed and you feel good.
Three. From head to toe, you are feeling perfect in every way.
On number four, your eyes begin to feel sparkling clear.
On the next number now, eyelids open, fully aware, feeling wonderfully good in every way.

Number five. Eyelids open, take a good deep breath, fill up your lungs and stretch.

How did you do?

Remember the rule: **if you had any response, you have been 100% successful.** You've got a response from your subconscious mind, if you had *any* of the following

- felt any part of your body relaxing
- noticed your breathing slowing down
- felt a light sensation in any part of your right hand or arm
- felt a heavy sensation in any part of your left hand or arm
- felt parts of your body jerking suddenly, as stored tension released
- felt your eyelids resist opening, whether they opened or not
- felt your hands resist unclasping, whether they unclasped or not
- thought it lasted a shorter time than it did
- thought it lasted a longer time than it did
- enjoyed the experience

Physical signs of trance

If you filmed yourself, look closely at your expression while in trance. If you looked sweet and innocent, maybe younger, that is known as the "hypnotic mask" – an absence of animation in the face, which is one of the signs of trance, and vanishes when the trance terminates. Some other signs of the trance are when the whites of your eyes become a little red, and your eyes leak tears, although you are not sobbing or crying.

Next chapter, next step

We have another phase of learning about trance yet to come, but first we'll note eight important principles of how your mind works. These have an all-important effect on how you learn, and whether what you learn becomes a real change. So pay attention!

Once you incorporate awareness of these eight principles into your practice, you are eight steps ahead and on your way to being a highly effective self-programmer.

RULES OF THE MIND

1. EVERY THOUGHT OR IDEA HAS A CORRESPONDING PHYSICAL REACTION.

2. WHAT IS EXPECTED TENDS TO BE REALIZED.

3. IMAGINATION IS ALWAYS MORE POWERFUL THAN REASON.

4. OPPOSING IDEAS CANNOT BE HELD AT ONE AND THE SAME TIME.

5. ONCE AN IDEA HAS BEEN ACCEPTED AT A SUBCONSCIOUS LEVEL, IT REMAINS THERE AND GOVERNS OUR BEHAVIOR IN THAT AREA OF OUR EXPRESSION FROM THAT TIME FORWARD UNTIL IT IS REPLACED BY A NEW IDEA, OR IS ALTERED AND AMENDED.

6. AN EMOTIONALLY INDUCED SYMPTOM PRODUCES ORGANIC CHANGE WHEN PERSISTED IN LONG ENOUGH.

7. EACH TIME YOUR NERVOUS SYSTEM REACTS IN A GIVEN WAY, IT BECOMES EASIER FOR IT TO REACT THAT WAY NEXT TIME.

8. WHEN DEALING WITH THE SUBCONSCIOUS MIND, THE GREATER THE CONSCIOUS EFFORT, THE LESS THE SUBCONSCIOUS RESPONSE.

Chapter 9

GETTING YOUR OWN MESSAGE - THE RULES OF THE MIND

So now that you've reached the point of being able to program yourself in trance, the next step is to learn this collection of principles that govern the operation of the mind, in particular the process of accepting new ideas. I have termed this collection of principles "The Rules of the Mind" and I will now state these rules in a simple way that will help you to internalize and accept them.

> **Rule 1: Every thought or idea has a corresponding physical reaction**

This rule is so well known in general life that we have many sayings in the language that refer to the reactions that we experience in our body in response to our thoughts. For example, we say, "He gives me a pain in the neck." Why would the pain develop in the neck? Because there are nerve centers activated by emotions, that trigger the muscles in the neck to become tense. Similarly, there is a great center of nerves in the solar plexus, and strong emotion can give us powerful sensations in the abdominal area.

You can think of many examples of how our language reflects the fact that our thoughts affect our bodies

"He/she/it makes me sick to my stomach".
"Just being around that person, I get a headache."
"Every time I think of how he/she broke my heart, tears just flood up into my eyes."

These familiar sayings are called **"Organ Language"** – an illustration that every thought or feeling creates a response in the body. Some of these things are quite evident. When you think an angry thought, the adrenal glands can become activated and adrenaline surges into your system. As a result, your heart will pump more quickly and a flush may come up into your face. When you think sad thoughts you feel a lump in your throat, and tears coming up into your eyes.

Sometimes you are aware of these physical effects and sometimes you're not. Just because you're not fully aware of the effects to the degree that you are when you have a certain feeling and then experience a definite effect that you consciously notice, such as a rapid heart beat or the tears in the eyes, doesn't mean that effects aren't being created.

We tend to think of problems and symptoms as mental or physical or emotional, and that's totally wrong. We are mental *and* physical *and* emotional. And those three aspects of the organism are operating synergistically all of the time, every minute of every day. The total effect of that interaction – the Whole – is always greater than the sum of the parts.

Thoughts are not separate from the rest of you.

The bottom line is that if you want to be healthy, to maintain your health, and to live longer, then you've got to discipline your mind to think appropriate thoughts as much and as often as you can.

As I mentioned at the beginning of this book, I don't use the term "positive thinking". I don't really know what it means, because I don't think it's possible, to have only positive thoughts in your mind. The realities of life include tragedies and difficulties, and it's not always appropriate for a human being to feel positive.

Grief, anger and acknowledgement of loss are part of the natural range of human emotions, and have their place in our lives. Often, they are the trigger for a significant learning process. What is important is that we do not call our attention to them unnecessarily, or dwell on them longer than is appropriate.

Let's take an example of how we can steer a healthy path through this. For instance, you can have a cut-off time some hours before you go to bed, when you don't watch any news or negative and disturbing content. You might want to get your news from a non-visual format, looking at words only.

Reading words doesn't produce the same kind of emotional response that watching images, particularly moving images, does. Although, for highly imaginative people, even just reading words can cause very intense images to be generated in their minds, and these images generate emotions and cause certain physical effects.

We often find sensible and healthy habit changes such as this, harder to make happen than we expect. This is where you can use trance and programming to make a difference.

> **Rule 2: What is expected tends to be realized.**

As we saw when we discussed the imagination, the **brain and nervous system respond only to mental images**. It doesn't matter whether the images are arising from your internal world or from the external world. If you imagine what you want to be and what you want to accomplish, you generate positive visual images and emotions that your subconscious mind cannot distinguish from actual experience. That can be very effective, because that daydream can be a kind of mental rehearsal. But here's a word of warning.

In and of itself mental rehearsal is not enough.

You won't find success just fantasizing about the day when you'll finally make it. But

Mental rehearsal can be very effective when action is added to it. What is expected tends to be realized.

One route by which **positive mental expectancy** often plays a role in success is when we need the cooperation of other people to get what we want, as they are likely to be influenced by our attitude. If we are relaxed and confident that people will like us, want to get to know us, and want to help us, this is likely to make them more likely to respond as we expect.

In the other direction, there are many routes by which negative expectations are reinforced into damaging and limiting habits.

Example: Many people use sickness to attract sympathy and attention. That seems paradoxical, because sympathy can often be a negative kind of emotion. I believe that sympathy, used as a non-empowering response, should only habitually be expressed to very small children and aged people. It doesn't give anything of a positive, inspirational nature, you see. It's a supportive kind of expression, and therefore it is weakening to people who can instead be encouraged to support themselves. It's not the same as empathy, which is a different kind of word, and expresses alliance and fellow-feeling, which can be both inspirational and encouraging.

Why would people settle for sympathy? What they really want is love and affection. But it's evident that *they don't believe they are worthy of love and instead they seek sympathy and attention* by being sick and/or suffering, and staying sick and/or suffering.

So what they expect is realized, they don't get love but get sympathy instead.

Example: Others will cling to their symptoms, be this illness or lack of success, or suffering in some other way, in an effort to punish themselves for real or imagined sins. Their guilt mounts to such a degree while waiting for God (their view of God) to punish them, that *because they believe they deserve punishment they generate illness or other suffering* as a way of punishing themselves. So what they expect is realized, they are punished.

Example: Sometimes it's to punish others. "I was a healthy and vigorous woman until I married you and look at what your running around and drinking has done to me. You've made a wreck of me. I hope you're satisfied." Why would someone suffer so much just to punish others? Because they *believe the power to fulfill their lives and achieve what they want lies with the other person,* not with themselves. So what they expect is realized, they have no power. This belief that you absolutely must control another person, because you yourself have no way of getting what you want directly, also leads to *manipulating others through creating guilt* concerning your physical or emotional distress.

Example: There is also the use of symptoms *to avoid responsibility*. This stems from *believing ourselves to be weak*, or at least believing that we must save all our effort for ourselves and so can't afford to waste it on helping others. So we say, "If only my back was okay, I could really help you in the garden," or "I'd give you a hand lifting that, but I can't help because of my back." This will often happen in relationships, where there is resentment and rejection of intimacy, and one party or the other may develop a physical symptom which prevents intimacy. What is expected is realized, they are always irresponsible and weak.

Using self-hypnosis can alter, amend, or even replace these ideas that are fixed in the subconscious mind and that are governing and controlling our behavior in that area of our expression.

> **Rule 3: Imagination is always more powerful than reason.**

Many people take great pride in their intellect and in the use of their reason. I often say that such a person has "the engineering mind," because engineers must deal with logic and reason in their work. But in dealing with our emotions and the emotions of those we relate to, rationality takes second place to imagination. We see this principle in action negatively when we experience inner conflict, for instance, our imagination giving us tempting ideas of over-indulgence generating powerful emotions of anticipated pleasure and satisfaction which often sweep aside our reasoned understanding that this would harm our health.

How do we use that principle creatively?

When you're in a trance, you can easily excite your imagination with creative and powerful programming. This means that you take positive ideas and concepts that you have created in accordance with the rules and principles that I'm teaching you now, and you combine them with your self-created hypnotic trance.

That process excites your imagination so that for perhaps the first time you are able to see yourself thinking, feeling, acting and behaving in the way that means to you the realization of your goals.

It causes your imagination to **become excited for your own benefit** so that you achieve your goals and experience the success you are seeking.

> **Rule 4: Opposing ideas cannot be held at one and the same time.**

This is a very important rule, so important that we'll have a section later in this book, about how to understand inner conflict, opposing ideas in your own mind causing friction and obstruction. To program ourselves effectively, that is not only to have ideas but to put them into action, we need to be aware of any opposing ideas that are pulling in the other direction.

This is one of the most common reasons for lack of effective response to programming – some parts of us have not signed on to the program. We've been "double-dealing" ourselves, and so we undermine our own efforts.

The most common inner conflict is between principle and temptation, that is, a conflict between a value that we officially sign up to, and taking opportunities that seem more convenient, profitable or pleasant at the time. This is often characterized in cartoons by the image of an angel on one shoulder and a devil on the other. We often vividly experience this kind of "cross-talk" in ourselves, and hear the many persuasive arguments that the "devil" uses to talk us out of our principles.

Example: You can talk about your own honesty and yet constantly compromise your principles by saying, "Well, it won't hurt to cheat just this one time," "It's for a good cause," "The end justifies the means," and all of those other rationalizations that compromise your principles and, of course, inherently compromise your honesty.

Example: Research shows that the effects of the use of some substances which are used as recreational drugs have powerful damaging effects on the brain and nervous system. Yet many people rationalize, "All that research is just generated by a bunch of people in the establishment who'll throw out any lie to get me to stop using drugs." There are opposing ideas here, on the one hand, they're saying, "The scientific world is good as long as it proposes ideas and principles that I and all of my peers want to hear." And on the other hand they're saying, "But if the scientific world reports something that I don't want to hear, then I would rather reject science and risk the consequences than to possibly have one of my friends say, 'What are you, some kind of sissy? Come on. Let's get high!'"

Example: An example here from my personal experience, life lesson learned! When I was young I was rebellious and didn't concern myself with what the rest of the world thought. I would have been far more successful in every way that success can be defined if I hadn't been so rebellious for so long. Despite the fact that your immediate circle of friends may condone such behavior at this moment in time, you can't be certain how your behavior will be received by others in the future, whose opinion will matter to you.

Awareness and Reflection in Programming

When programming yourself for real, powerful and lasting change, you've got to know what your thoughts are and how you're going to deal with them. You're not an island. You also have to consider what the rest of the world thinks and how it's going to react, and how you're going to deal with that.

Compromise causes conflict

That's the consequence of compromising principle. That's the price that you pay, because that conflict creates certain unavoidable mental, physical and emotional symptoms within you. And you can't always know what consequences will arise when you compromise your basic principles. So when you're creating your programming, make sure that you only include statements that you can 100% sign up to. As you progress, what you can 100% sign up to will expand and increase.

> **Rule 5: Once an idea has been accepted at a subconscious level, it remains there and governs our behavior in that area of our expression from that time forward until it is replaced by a new idea or is altered or amended.**

The companion or "flipside" to rule five states, *The longer the idea remains, the more difficult it is to replace it with a new idea*, because we develop a pattern of reaction in that area. If the longer an idea remains, the more difficult it is to replace it with a new idea, there is an obvious question that arises, "If limiting ideas and principles governing my behavior were accepted back there when I was three, four, five or six years old, and I'm thirty-seven years old now, won't I have a lot of trouble changing them?"

All human beings resist change because of **habituation** and because of fear. They resist change until they reach a point of **readiness for change**. The only thing we want to avoid is, having to spend a lifetime to reach the point of readiness for change. Let's get there and let's get it done. We can't get into orbit until we're first on the launching pad and then we must press that button that fires up the rockets.

Let's review the sequence in which **patterns of reaction** are formed. First comes the thought, followed by the feeling, followed by the action. Then comes the habit of *thinking* that thought in that situation, the habit of *feeling* that feeling *in that situation*, and the habit of *acting* that way in *that situation*. Let's consider some very common thoughts that lead to the types of patterns of reaction that then become problems.

Example – social situations: Some people think that they've got to have a drink to "steady their nerves" in situations where they feel they must make a good impression on others. The situation may be an audition, or a job interview, or a party. If I were to ask any representative group the questions, "Are you a friendly person?", "Are you a social person?" They'd be likely to say, "Oh, sure I am!" If I say, "Tell me, when you go to a party, do you just walk right up to new people you want to get acquainted with and say, 'Hi. I'm X. What's your name?' and just start getting acquainted with them?" Chances are the answer would be, "Yes, I like to do that." But the question is not, "Do you like to do it?" I know they like to do it. The question is, "Do you start right out and do it?" And often the answer is, "Oh, sure I do. I just like to have a few drinks first." Or perhaps they say they would like to smoke a joint first. I had an uncle who liked to "steady his nerves" like that. The last time I saw him, he got so "steady" he didn't move for two days!

Example – creativity: Think for just a moment of some of the self-destructive patterns of reaction that people have come to believe to be a necessary part of their creativity. We can all think of great musicians and other performers who are no longer with us, or became a shadow of themselves, through believing that they could only be creative if they used drugs and alcohol. Now it's true that alcohol and other drugs are indeed stimulants at first. And it can seem as though artificial stimulants are an answer to the challenge of sparking one's creativity. But it's obvious that the continuing effect is self-destructive. All the evidence provided by those who have gone before testifies to the fact that reliance upon artificial stimulants is ultimately self-destructive and is a form of anti-life behavior. Yet the belief that these substances are an answer to the challenges of life remains. And **the more often you give in to the belief, the more powerful the belief becomes.**

Time to Choose

I'll give you another example from my own experience. I made a choice to change a habit. My choice then is the reason I'm here today.

Many years ago, I used to work in nightclubs performing hypnosis on stage. And when I worked in places such as Las Vegas, I did from seventeen to twenty shows a week. On weekends I did three and four shows an evening. Along about the fourth show, I'd sometimes think, "Well, I'll just have a drink tonight to give me a little energy." Then I found I was ordering doubles. And then instead of just doing it for the last show, I was doing it for the last two shows.

Finally it came to me and I said, "If I'm doing this now and I'm just in my early thirties, how's it going to be later on? If I can't find within myself the power to go out on that floor with the excitement and energy and enthusiasm that when I say, 'Good evening, ladies and gentlemen!' every single person in that theater knows that I'm going to be dynamite that night, then I can't be an entertainer. If I can't cope with all the events of my life and sweep them aside as I step on that stage, then I'm not a professional. I can't be in the business of entertaining others if I have to rely upon an artificial stimulant." And I just stopped.

Working in show business, I saw around me many examples of people who had either never got to that point of choice, or chosen the other path. You can see that although it happened in an instant, it was a profound moment. I had two versions of myself before me, and I had to choose one.

When you are self-programming, the more vividly you set out the version of yourself that you want in the future, the more powerful your commitment will be.

> **Rule 6: An emotionally induced symptom produces organic change when persisted in long enough.**

> **Rule 7: Each time your nervous system reacts in a given way, it becomes easier for it to react that way the next time.**

These are twin rules, because if you do something for long enough, it creates a semi-automatic process in your nervous system and eventually causes a permanent shift in how your nervous system functions. Once this shift takes place, then any function or organ in the body can be affected.

The effects of your thoughts on your body build up over time. If you are **chronically** involved in worry, if you are chronically involved in expecting the worst, if you are chronically involved in catastrophic expectations, then you're going to suffer the effects in your body. There are powerful effects of stress, for instance, on the immune system, which can weaken your resistance to infection and illness.

It is easier to control a symptom while it's still a functional symptom, as if organic damage has occurred as a result, there's much more work to do. Once a habit is formed, it becomes easier to follow and much more difficult to break. When you begin doing something different, you're establishing a new pattern in neural pathways in the brain.

When you stop doing something, you're withdrawing from the old patterns of neural pathways in the brain. When you begin with self-hypnosis, much of what you're doing is often said to be undoing or breaking old habit patterns. The word "breaking" is really an inappropriate word because

You don't "break" old habit patterns.
You begin new habit patterns.

With self-hypnosis, you can much more easily establish these new habits and patterns.

> Rule 8: When dealing with the subconscious mind, the greater the conscious effort, the less the subconscious response.

In other words, if you want to maximize your subconscious response, you don't grit your teeth and try hard, because the harder you try, the less result you get. You must learn a pattern of letting it happen. You allow it to happen instead of trying to make it happen. You step aside and allow yourself to respond independently of conscious effort.

For some people, this can be a difficult thing to do at first. It's really a very simple thing to do, but if you are one of those individuals who have certain kinds of fearful responses, it can be very difficult. If you have a deep fear of what might happen if you didn't maintain control at all times, it can be very difficult for you not to get caught up in trying to *make* the response happen by using your conscious mind, because in order to let the response originate from within your subconscious mind, you must let go of conscious control and allow control to revert to a more powerful part of yourself.

You see, you use your conscious mind to determine the nature of the response that you wish to evoke from your subconscious mind, but when it comes time to experience that subconscious response, it is necessary for you to turn control over to your subconscious and to allow that part of yourself to control your response.

People often say to me, "Isn't the hypnotist controlling the person who is being hypnotized?" Not at all. If the hypnotist could somehow create the subconscious responses that we see occurring within you in hypnosis, we could then say that the hypnotist is controlling you. But hypnotic suggestion merely communicates to you what the hypnotist wants your subconscious mind to do, and your subconscious mind then controls the response for you.

In hypnosis, you appear to give up control, but what you are really doing is shifting control from the conscious level to another part of yourself. That's why you achieve more powerful results when you allow the conscious mind and the subconscious mind to work together than you achieve when the conscious mind is trying to work by itself, and far more powerful than when the conscious mind is trying to work against the opposition of the subconscious mind.

If you can't relax whenever you want to, if you can't go to sleep whenever you want to, if you can't let go whenever you want to, then you are <u>not</u> in control. You're not in control because you're unable to relinquish control. You're unable to surrender control. You are overcontrolled. You're suffering from a compulsion to control, which is always based upon fear.

> **Self-hypnosis can bring you to a place where perhaps for the first time in your life, *you* are exercising control over you.**

Chapter 10

TRANCE "SECRETS" - TWO ROUTES, FIVE METHODS

How do you feel at this stage, about your own ability to respond to trance induction? If you still feel a bit of inhibition, that's okay. Inhibition doesn't mean, "I'm determined to prove that I can't be hypnotized." It means, "I want to respond, but I have a feeling that I probably won't". As long as you are willing to practice your self-hypnosis routine on a regular basis, then you condition yourself for future response to self-hypnosis each time you do it.

Remember that there are no chance, or random factors, involved. Hypnosis works on certain principles, and just as surely as when you exercise a muscle regularly, it gets stronger, when you practice self-hypnosis regularly, you respond more and more. The principle involved is that **hypnotic trance happens when an effect occurs in the central nervous system**, and there are only two major ways you can do this.

Route 1: Understimulation

You can fatigue and tire the nervous system by the presentation of monotonous, repetitive ideas presented in a certain cadence of sound patterns, intonations, and frequencies. You experienced fatiguing of the nervous system as the approach being used in our practice earlier, when the relaxing suggestions were given in a slow, sonorous tone (you'll notice this particularly if you used my recordings).

You'll remember that in those suggestions I utilized the repetition of ideas of sleep, rest and relaxation occurring over and over again. The repetition of those ideas, in the absence of stimulation, fatigues the nervous system. Eventually, because there's no new content to those repetitive ideas to stimulate your attention, your conscious mind becomes fatigued and just steps aside, you see. That's why I say, "Don't try to concentrate on what I'm saying." How can you concentrate when there's no content? Therefore, if you're concentrating, you're really struggling to prevent yourself letting go.

Route 2: Overstimulation

The other way is to overload the nervous system by giving it enough stimulation so that it goes into trance or "checks out" in order to give itself a break. As well as in times of sensory overload, this often occurs naturally in, for instance, people involved in serious accidents or other traumatic circumstances. If you have understanding of trance, when you see someone in a state of shock, you recognize a key characteristic of trance is present – that is, the critical faculty is partially or completely inactive at that time. In that state, they are often receptive to suggestion, and knowledge of suggestion can be very helpful in dealing with them, as they often cannot effectively manage normal conscious communication.

In order to demonstrate to students that trance can be induced by overstimulation, I use a number of methods which are totally harmless, but involve this principle. For instance, I might use a loud command, and as the nervous energy peaks upward in response, I would rapidly give a suggestion that they will relax, and as the critical faculty is not active in that moment due to the response, the energy drops just as rapidly, and they are in a trance. Although it looks dramatic, there is nothing mysterious about it. It all has a valid explanation, and understanding this will help you to make the most of any occasions when your critical faculty is by-passed, even through circumstances beyond your control.

The Five Trance Methods

There are only five main principles underlying the methods involved in producing a trance. All five don't have to occur together, they can occur singly or in combination. Again, there is film of me demonstrating these methods.

Trance Method 1: Startling Command

The first method by which trance can be produced involves the use of a startling command. The startling command overloads the nervous system, the conscious mind steps aside, and trance is produced. Usually the command I use is SLEEP! Trance is not sleep, but your nervous system is already familiar with the word sleep, and will respond by setting aside the critical faculty and relaxing, which occurs in sleep, and is what we want.

Trance Method 2: Loss of Equilibrium

The second method by which trance can be produced involves developing the loss of equilibrium in full or in part. I often demonstrate this by taking the hand of the person I'm hypnotizing and pulling them towards me, at the same time asking them to let their body just come forward, until they are leaning against me. I can then bring them upright, and they have still let go of their equilibrium, they don't try to restore it. That helps just to push aside the critical faculty of the conscious mind.

You can have a partial loss, as when the person lets go and leans against me, or a complete loss of equilibrium. If I want to demonstrate a complete loss of equilibrium, I would get someone to stand behind the person I'm hypnotizing without their being aware of it, and then suddenly push them backward and over into the arms of the catcher while shouting the startling command, SLEEP! at the same time. Their whole body will just sway over backward and be caught and lowered down. I don't recommend you try this unless you've been expertly trained! It's dramatic as a demonstration, but it's not necessary to have a completely loss of equilibrium, you can use a partial loss of equilibrium just as effectively.

Partial loss of equilibrium can be achieved through any means that momentarily alters the center of gravity. It can be done with a handshake that draws the body forward, or it can be done having the person press their right hand against my right hand, so that they're applying a good, steady pressure. When I remove my hand suddenly, their body moves forward and they lose equilibrium and trance can be rapidly induced. This can be done in a seated position also.

It is not, of course, possible for you to use these demonstration methods on yourself, and **they are not suitable for use without being trained under expert guidance**. In other words, do not do this at home.

But if you find yourself swinging in a hammock, or floating in water, or feeling physically "shaken up" in some way, say in a fairground ride, you can recognize it as a trance method, relax, and even program yourself.

Trance Method 3: Misdirection

There are two types of misdirection: physical misdirection and mental misdirection.

Physical misdirection is often used in entertainment hypnosis. It involves using natural physical phenomena as a method of convincing a person that they are hypnotized. As soon as they are convinced of this, of course, they are hypnotized! An example would be a hypnotist asking a person to interlock the fingers of both hands, while holding their arms out in front of them, with the palms facing outwards, then asking them to raise their arms over their head, and try to pull hands apart. Because of the opposing muscular forces involved, there is a lot of resistance to this, however if the hypnotist does it with enough showmanship, the person is convinced they must be hypnotized, as they can't pull their hands apart. This is different from the hand-locking test we used earlier, where the hands were positioned differently, and could be easily pulled apart if not for the counter-suggestion.

Mental misdirection is different from mental confusion, which is a separate technique. To mentally misdirect simply means to misdirect the focus of your mental awareness. This is used very effectively by illusionist "magicians" on stage, when they distract your attention from the fact that they are slipping something into their pocket, by at the same time producing a bunch of flowers from within their sleeve, for example. You were looking at the flowers instead. That's misdirected attention.

Attention can be misdirected in any of a number of ways and, while the conscious mind is focusing its attention where we have directed it, we catch it off guard, so to speak, and put in the suggestion for trance while the critical faculty is inattentive.

In self-hypnosis, we can use this to by-pass a resistance to respond, for instance, by directing the attention to a brightly visualized scene, while we give suggestions for trance or programming.

This is one of the most widely-used methods in hypnosis, to direct the mind to relaxing or pleasant scenes in the imagination, while the programming goes on. We'll learn more about this later, as it is a useful method in self-hypnosis.

Trance Method 4: Mental Confusion

Mental confusion is separate and distinct from mental misdirection. In mental misdirection, the conscious attention is directed upon a specific focus. In mental confusion, the conscious attention is made to shift between a number of different things so that confusion results. Mental confusion gains its effectiveness from the fact that you don't really know where to settle your mind. First you think, "Well is it this?" then, "Is it that?" and finally, "What's going on?"

The conscious mind becomes involved in attempting to analyze the confusion. At that point you slip in your suggestion to sleep. The suggestion reaches the subconscious mind because you are slipping it past the critical faculty while it's busy trying to figure out the nature of the confusion. These are deliberate tactics that can be brought into play to confuse your mind.

The only time I use mental confusion is when I encounter someone with a form of resistance that is difficult to deal with and I want to penetrate that resistance quickly. Then I'll combine mental confusion with some of the other principles.

With self-hypnosis, you can take advantage of mentally confusing and exhausting situations, by slipping into a trance state, provided your conscious attention is not urgently required. Your critical faculty will be glad of the opportunity for a break.

Trance Method 5: Relaxation

Finally, the fifth method by which trance can be produced is relaxation. This approach involves inducing a trance through the process of fractional relaxation, which you're now familiar with because it's the one we used before in our trance practice.

This relaxation principle is the most common way in which we induce trance for self-hypnosis.

Combinations

Relaxation and misdirection (or redirection) of attention are often combined, for instance, in visualizing a scene that has relaxing and pleasant associations for you, while including suggestions for physical and mental relaxation. It can be fun and also a useful exercise, to create vivid visualizations of this kind.

Safe Place

A common use of this combination is a technique known as the "safe place", where you create a **visualization of a place that is special to you** – it can be real, from your memory, or imaginary, from a book, for instance (remember as long as the image is vivid, the central nervous system will respond to an image whether internally or externally generated). Once you have created this vivid visualization in your mind, and practiced it in trance until a habit pattern is formed, you can recall it very rapidly by connecting it in your mind to a trigger such as counting and snapping your fingers, or pressing the tips of your thumb and forefinger together, for instance, and you have an immediate relaxing effect and move into trance. You can also use it as a deepener if you are already in trance, or to give yourself a pleasant experience at the end of a programming session.

Mental Expectancy based on Understanding

As you see, it's not a mystery. As an entertainment hypnotist, one might make it appear mysterious so that the audience asked, "I wonder how that was done?" An entertainment hypnotist often deliberately capitalizes on the mystery surrounding hypnosis, because as the conscious mind comes to accept a process as mysterious, disbelief is suspended. As a result, mental expectancy is then more easily generated and directed toward specific ends.

In explaining these principles to you, I'm doing the opposite. Rather than seeking to mystify you, I'm hoping that you've now reached a point where you are thinking, "Now that I understand what hypnosis is all about and how it works, and now that I realize that what we're dealing with here is a natural state of mind, I guess it will work for me, too." If you're thinking this, you're right! So when your critical faculty steps aside, you enter trance and the hypnotic contract is in place. When this becomes habitual and familiar to you, **your positive mental expectancy about trance becomes part of your everyday thinking.**

Depth of Trance

It's likely that you're getting deeper and deeper in trance each time you practice. If you are, this is wonderful. If you're not, this is also fine.

> **Depth of trance is very pleasant, but it doesn't directly relate to response to programming for change.**

Various degrees of trance exist, but in self-hypnosis it is **your responsibility to develop the fullness of your own responsiveness.** You do that by your continued practice, ideally every day at the same time and in the same place. That is important because each time the nervous system responds in a given way, it becomes easier for it to react that way the next time. **You're developing patterns of reaction.**

Chapter 11

A FULL PROGRAMMING SESSION – ON CONFIDENCE

This time you're going to experience what a full programming session is like. You'll see that it's like an encouraging, inspiring story that you tell yourself about yourself. There are some rules about how you tell it, for maximum effectiveness, that I'll explain in a later chapter. Remember, first we show, then we tell! This time, the programming is about Confidence, because I find that more people want to learn self-hypnosis to increase confidence than any other goal.

Preparation

Get yourself comfortable lying down with pillows on the floor, or lying on your bed or couch. If you are not able to lie down, sit back comfortably. In your practice, you are becoming conditioned into a rapid response to the command, "sleep now", so I'm going to use that to induce trance rapidly, and then move on to deepening methods. *The deepening method used in this session is a visualization of walking down ten steps. If you don't like to walk down steps, you can go down on an escalator, in an elevator, or down or along a gently-sloping path, each time with the journey in ten segments, and accompanying suggestions for deepening.*

***Play recording/read aloud:**

<u>Induction:</u> *Now fix your eyes on a spot on the ceiling overhead. Stare at that spot without moving a muscle. Now take a deep breath and fill up your lungs. Exhale slowly, sleep now. Now a second and even deeper breath, exhale, sleep now. Now a third deep breath. Sleep now. Now just let your eyelids close down. Let each muscle and nerve*

begin to grow loose, and limp, and lazy, as you are relaxing more, with each sound that you hear, with each easy breath that you take.

<u>Deepener – Expectancy/Preparation:</u> *I'm going to count from ten down to one, and as I do, I want you to imagine that you're walking down a flight of steps. With each number that I count, the quality of your deep relaxation becomes more profound. When I reach the count of one, you'll then be aware that you're enjoying a very pleasant state of hypnotic relaxation.*

<u>Deepener:</u> *Number ten, you take the first step downward, as each muscle and each nerve grows loose and limp and relaxed.*
Number nine, the wave of relaxation spreads all across your body.
Number eight, you're relaxing more with each easy breath that you take.
Number seven, every muscle and every nerve is growing so loose, and so limp, and so relaxed.
Number six, you're moving down, toward a new and deeper level of hypnotic relaxation, and on
Number five, you're halfway down now, and when I reach the count of one, I'll say the words, sleep deeply. You'll then be aware that you're more deeply relaxed than ever before.
Number four, each muscle and nerve lets loose, relaxing, you're drifting down, deeper and deeper in sleep.
Number three, going down, deeper in drowsy relaxation.
Number two, on the next number, I'll give the signal, I'll say the words, sleep deeply. When I do, you'll then be aware that you're enjoying a very profound state of hypnotic relaxation.
Number one, sleep deeply. Now just relax, and go deeper into hypnosis.

<u>Programming:</u> *As you go deeper into relaxation, you are realizing that you are a constantly growing and maturing personality. You are becoming aware of the strengths and abilities that have developed within you. You feel a sense of confidence in your ability to achieve*

the goals you've chosen for yourself, for you are learning to believe in yourself.

You appreciate yourself and you do good and kind things for yourself. You meet each situation as it comes with calm and quiet assurance. You are making contact with the center of wisdom and power within you, which knows what to do and how to do it. Whatever you say, whatever you do, is said and done with complete confidence and self-assurance.

You walk with a spring in your step. Your head is held high and you see the beauty of life around you. People respect you because you respect them and you respect yourself. You have confidence in your own judgment. You are honest and dependable. You can and you do move forward from one positive achievement to another.

People are aware that you like them. They sense your goodwill. You are cheerful and enthusiastic, and you attract friends because you are friendly. You are sincere and honest, and your personal integrity is felt by everyone you meet.

You are becoming free, for you are now discovering the truth about yourself and the world around you. You are free to act. Your body is yours to direct in positive action. Your emotional power is yours to use creatively and constructively, for you have the power to choose and the power to act. You are active, alive, and aware, letting the power and energy of your subconscious mind surge through you as perfect ideas and creative activity.

You are developing a belief in yourself, a belief in your fellow man, a belief in the honesty and integrity of the laws of life, for you are unique. Never before has life been expressed through any other person in exactly the same way it is now being expressed through you. You are important to life. You have special qualifications. There are things for you to do that can and should be done better by you than by any other person.

You live in such a way that you approve of yourself. You now know that life can bring every good thing to you. Through your imagination, through your creative thinking, you are now directing your life into full and complete expression. You know that you can do what you're designed to do in the best possible way, for you love life, and you express life in a wholesome and positive way.

Each day you meet new and interesting people, and as you approach people for the first time, you feel a warmth and friendship for them. Your smile and your friendly greetings express your sincere feelings toward them. You enjoy being with people. You are poised and confident when talking with new acquaintances or with good friends.

People enjoy being with you because you are so alive and so vibrant. You are secure, relaxed, and poised when you are with people. You easily and gratefully accept the warm friendship that people offer you, for you truly deserve it. You enjoy people and you want to do things for them. You know that people seek you out because you are unique and you enjoy their acceptance of you. People respond to your personal integrity, and your special personality and warm friendliness draw people close to you just as a magnet attracts iron filings.

You're a happy person full of imaginative thoughts, which pour forth from you constantly. Each day you feel more lovable, more interesting, and you're becoming more interested in others. You recognize and accept the friendship that people offer you, for you deserve it. You have a deep and sincere respect for yourself and for your personal worth to others.

It is easy for you to accept the help and cooperation of others. You see their help to you as an expression of mutual friendship and understanding. You realize that giving and receiving are two sides of a single coin. You're aware of the trust and confidence you generate in others and it makes you feel good.

You think of yourself as a warm, generous and loving person. You easily express love and affection, and you find it easy to accept love and approval from others. You like yourself because you are a friendly and giving person. You accept yourself as a unique and valuable person.

You are open, honest and direct in your relations with people. You recognize that you are talented and creative and this awareness makes you feel good. You express your creativity in the interests and the activities that you pursue. You allow yourself time for your special interests, time for your personal recreation, and time for your programmed relaxation.

You now release and forgive everyone who has ever hurt you in the past. You bless them and, in your imagination, you wish for them the very same good you wish for yourself. You now forgive yourself for your mistaken attitudes and actions of the past. You now know that every mistake that you have ever made, as you understand it, becomes a stepping-stone to greater understanding and greater opportunity. You give the best of yourself and only the best of life comes back to you. You feel gratified and fulfilled to be the special person that you truly are.

<u>Post-hypnotic suggestion:</u> *Now, each of these ideas has made a vivid, deep, and permanent impression on your subconscious mind. And each day in your daily life you become more and more aware of the full, powerful, creative expression of these ideas.*

<u>Trance Termination Expectancy/Preparation:</u> *Now, I'm going to count from one to five, and then I'll say, "Fully aware". At the count of five, your eyes are open, you're fully aware then, feeling calm, rested, refreshed and relaxed.*

<u>Trance Termination:</u> *All right.*

One. Slowly, calmly, easily, and gently you are returning to your full awareness once again.
Two. Each muscle and nerve in your body is loose and limp and relaxed, and you feel wonderfully good.
Three. From head to toe you're feeling perfect in every way — physically perfect, mentally perfect, emotionally calm and serene.
On number four, your eyes begin to feel sparkling clear, just as though they were bathed in cold spring water.
On the next number I count, eyelids open, fully aware, feeling calm, rested, refreshed, relaxed, invigorated, and full of energy.
Number five. You're fully aware now. Eyelids open. Take a deep breath, fill up your lungs, and stretch.

How did you do?

As you listened to the programming, you may have had one or more of the following experiences

1. You were relaxing so deeply the words flowed over you and you didn't react to their content and meaning.

2. You were aware of the words at least some of the time, and let them flow over you.

3. You were aware of the words at least some of the time, and felt accepting of them, welcoming their message and meaning.

4. You were aware of the words at least some of the time, and felt a reaction, doubt or disbelief, at the message and meaning of at least some of them.

If you had experiences 1, 2 or 3, you will most probably benefit from regular confidence programming along these lines.

If you had experience 4, let's look at what might be happening and how you can work with that experience.

Chapter 12

FIVE WAYS THAT GIVE US CONFIDENCE IN IDEAS

Over and over again, I hear people who come to me for self-hypnosis say, "I lost my confidence", "I never had any confidence", "I need to gain confidence". *All of these statements are false.* The reason is

You were born with confidence.

You came into this world with great confidence. When your diaper was wet or you were hungry, you made a loud noise until someone came and took care of it. I'm sure you know people who go through a lifetime and never learn any other method for filling their needs. They just keep making a loud noise and hope that someone will come and take care of it. It's called *manipulating the environment.* It's perfectly appropriate when you're lying there in the crib, because you haven't yet developed the strength and power within yourself to fill your needs in any measure. But it's certainly not appropriate for the adult!

People are confident – about the wrong things.

Every one of you has a great deal of confidence. Hundreds of students and clients have said to me, for instance, "I just can't seem to be relaxed when I take an examination. I tense up. The things I've studied do not seem to be available in my memory. I don't know what it is." They say this to me WITH GREAT CONFIDENCE. They have great confidence in the way they're going to behave when they take an examination.

CONFIDENCE IN THE WRONG THINGS AFFECTS YOUR PERFORMANCE.

Have you ever said, for instance, "I just can't speak in public. I freeze up in front of a group of people" or "I'm no good at introducing myself to new people. I feel they won't be interested in me"? We have great confidence in this kind of belief about ourselves – we've repeated these statements to ourselves many, many times.

Now, consider this: Every time you say, "I just can't speak in public" or "I'm no good at introducing myself", which of the following results takes place

1. That thought or statement tremendously improves your ability to speak in public or to introduce yourself, or

2. It doesn't have any effect because it's only words and thoughts, or

3. Each time you think, "I can't speak in public", "I can't introduce myself", it further inhibits your ability to speak in public or to introduce yourself.

If you answered number three, give yourself an A!

We are confident that we will *not* succeed

When you understand this process of self-programming, it becomes obvious what happens as a result of our misplaced confidence. Yes, in our daily lives we each have areas in which we are totally confident that we're *not* going to succeed.

We can, for instance, have great confidence that in a meaningful relationship we're going to be rejected sooner or later. Because we fear that we're *unlovable*.

We can "know" that in a given situation we're going to make a fool of ourselves. We say, "When I stand up to speak in front of people, I'm going to say the wrong thing and everyone is going to laugh at me. I know that because it happened to me in the second grade. When the teacher told me to recite a verse we'd learned, I couldn't do it and everyone laughed at me. I've been holding it right in my mind ever since. I've made up my mind that I'm never going to stand up in front of people again and feel humiliated and embarrassed. Now I'm an adult, and I'm still avoiding speaking in public."

Liberation and Transformation of Energy

Behavior is simply the expression of energy. For a long time the scientific view was that the universe was made up of two elements, matter and energy. But Albert Einstein discovered that there is no such thing as matter, separate from energy – there is only energy. He discovered that although our human senses might not always perceive it, all material objects are actually composed of energy. If we could penetrate to the very heart of material objects, we would find energy and movement. Energy is the basis of our behavior.

> The way we behave in any situation is the release of the energy that we have linked to that situation.

Example: Much of our behavior is habitual and habits are energy patterns. We may get up each morning and brush our teeth because we want to care for our teeth so that we might have them for a longer time. Our teeth-brushing reflects our care for ourselves and our knowledge that our bodies need taking care of.

So to make a change, your energy, in the form of confidence, has to move from the belief in failure to the belief in success, that is, we're going to deal with the **liberation** of energy and the **transformation** of energy. We must first liberate it from the places where it is invested and is acting to affect you in ways that cause your behavior to be counterproductive, unsatisfying and frustrating.

How Energy becomes invested in Ideas

What makes us behave in a particular situation a certain way, the same way every time, even though we've come to recognize that this behavior is unsatisfying and even counterproductive?

We can all think of examples, from our own behavior and that of those we know.

- Many people take out a gym membership and despite the fact that they have paid the membership fee, rarely attend to exercise despite their intention to do so.

- Many people decide to go on a diet, tape the eating program to the door of the fridge, buy the required foods, and end up eating take-out after a day and a half.

- In interactions with others, the same unsatisfactory patterns are often repeated again and again, despite our saying to ourselves, "I won't let them get under my skin", "I'll be understanding and tolerant" or "I'll stand up for myself next time".

- Long-term goals such as gaining a qualification, achieving career promotion or traveling to a place we've always wanted to go, are postponed again and again, always remaining on a horizon that doesn't get any closer.

These patterns show us that we have developed a habitual response to a particular stimulus. It may be the thought of going to the gym, eating the prescribed diet meal, interacting with others, or achieving that long-term goal – whatever it is, we are responding to these things, or to what they symbolize to us. As a result we behave in a way that is contrary to the way we intellectually determine that we would like to behave. So there is some other type of thinking guiding our behavior, something we are usually either not conscious of, or only partly conscious of, and so it is called, "**deeply fixed ideas**".

> **Energy expressed as behavior acquires its character from fixed ideas held in the deeper level of the mind.**

The reason we call this deeper part of the mind the "subconscious mind" is that although we can become aware, or be dimly aware, of the ideas that it contains, we are often not fully aware of them and of their influence on our behavior. So, we can be frustrated and puzzled by our own actions, that are contrary to our conscious decisions. We start acquiring those fixed ideas from very early in our lives, as the parts of our mind that can form these ideas are present from infancy.

Deeply fixed ideas don't have to be as a result of trauma. Quite often these fixed ideas are simply our interpretation of our experiences. Early in our lives, we are very open to learning from many sources – we need to put together a picture of our world and our place in it, so that we can operate in it. So we make interpretations from many sources and incorporate them into our world picture. Some of these interpretations may not be correct even for the situation we're in, some may not work well in situations other than the one we're in, or they may have worked well for a child but don't work well for an adult.

When fixed ideas are unnecessarily limiting for us, because they prevent us from developing, expanding or fulfilling our hopes, they are called "limiting fixed ideas". Not all fixed ideas are limiting, but these are the ones that we tend to focus on in hypnosis, because they are preventing change and progress.

Programming

Let's look first at one of the main ways in which we acquire these deeply fixed ideas – **programming**. As young children, we are easily programmed because we haven't yet developed a critical faculty. So when a parent says to a child, "Why are you so bad," **that's a programming statement**. The question is actually a statement that says, "You are so bad. Tell me why." The child can only think, "I don't know", but the idea that they are bad has got into their mind.

This type of programming is known as an "**attribution**". The parent attributes a quality to the child, stated as though it is a description of the way the child actually is. This can be suggested as an *innate* quality, or even more confusing to the child, as a quality that they have chosen to display, so they are deserving of blame. Often, the child does not feel that they have made a choice, so they lose faith in their own judgment and sense of themselves, and accept the programmed version instead.

In this example, the idea programmed into the child's mind acquires its power in two ways.

First, there is the fact that idea is presented by the parent, who is an **authority figure**. The authority figure has power from the facts of the child's experience that this person wields control over them, and seems to understand the world, as they are able to deal with all sorts of things that the child does not understand, and they supply the child's material needs.

Second, the authority figure is attributing a quality to the child by **presenting it as a fact** about that child. How can the child argue against that?

Obviously, there are many limiting ideas that can become fixed in this manner. As the child goes to school, other ideas that are presented may be, "Why don't you do well in sports/ have more friends/ do well in reading?" The question, "Why don't you do well..." is really a statement, "You don't do well. Tell me why." This idea develops through **repetition** into a pattern, and the pattern becomes the problem – **a habit** rooted in deeply fixed ideas.

Fixed ideas give the character to our behavior. These fixed ideas come together to form concepts, which in turn are merged together to form attitudes. We can say that our fixed ideas determine our attitudes about ourselves, about the world around us, and the way in which we relate to the world.

Self Perception

Some people refer to the "**self image**", which relates to the way that we see ourselves. But I prefer the term "**self perception**", because it's a dynamic process. Sometimes, a perception can be a great awakening, and so we see instances where a person has a perception, which from that moment on changes the direction of their lives. More usually, our changes in perception are gradual, adapting to our new experiences. As our perception is altered and our awareness increases, we alter or replace ideas that were appropriate (or the best we could find then) in the past, but are not appropriate in the present.

In healthy thinking, we adapt and improve our perceptions as we go along in life. But this healthy, adaptive process doesn't always happen. I've often had people say, for instance, 'I had a threatening and punitive parent who told me, 'Open your mouth and I'll knock you over' so I learned to be passive." Or, "I had a threatening parent and so I learned to be defiant. I seethe with defiance, and now I have to defy all of the time."

To decide, "I have to be passive all the time", is an adaption that suited the child, because to be other than passive and submissive was very threatening, but it does not suit the adult. As a passive adult they are exploited. People recognize their unwillingness to assert themselves, to say, "I am not willing to be treated in that manner." Equally, an overly-aggressive adult is likely to alienate people and miss opportunities.

FIVE KEY PRINCIPLES IN ACCEPTING IDEAS

There are actually only a few key principles involved when we accept some ideas and reject others, and we do not do so through consideration of evidence and reasoned argument. That is, when our subconscious accepts these ideas, by-passing the critical faculty.

Key Principle 1: AUTHORITY FIGURE

We are much more likely to accept an idea at a subconscious level when it is presented by an authority figure.

An authority figure is anyone we consider to be smarter or more powerful than we are. It doesn't have to be anyone older or better educated. The authority figure could be a spouse or someone with whom you have an emotional relationship. In the case of a friendship, it is through the emotional relationship that friends come to influence each other.

> **Key Principle 2: EMOTIONALIZED**
>
> **Any idea that is accompanied by strong feelings or emotion is much more likely to be accepted at a subconscious level.**

Emotion is to the mind as light is to the camera. It sensitizes and opens the mind and allows that image to be come fixed.

It can be any emotion. It doesn't have to be a negative emotion. You can also create and engender positive and powerful ideas in a very emotional way that will overcome the negative programming of the past.

Unfortunately, in our childhood programming, the strongest emotions may be negative, with parents whose most intense emotional expression towards us is when criticizing or punishing us.

There are parents, of course, who do celebrate the positive achievements. But for people who have problems due to limiting fixed ideas, the emotional energy is attached to what you *don't* do. It's attached to what you're having difficulty with. It's attached to what you're failing to do. And that emotion fixes the limiting ideas.

> **Key Principle 3: REPETITION**
>
> **Any idea that is experienced repeatedly is much more likely to be accepted at a subconscious level.**

In the adult mind, the great storehouse of ideas and interpretations that we call the critical faculty of the conscious mind examines incoming ideas critically before accepting them.

The first step in the examination of an incoming idea is to attempt to link the idea with something that we have previously experienced, analyzed or worked with. If we can't make such an association, we tend to dismiss the new idea. That's why it's so very difficult for the adult mind to accept new ideas the first time we're exposed to them.

Throughout the conditioning process of repetition, these ideas gradually lose their newness. As we are repeatedly exposed to new ideas, we can focus on them more and begin to process them and accept them. It is the conditioning factor of repetition that greatly increases the acceptance of ideas.

> **Key Principle 4: MULTIPLE SOURCES**
>
> **An idea tends to be accepted more readily when it has been presented through multiple sources of reinforcement.**

If, for instance, an idea is presented by your parents and is reinforced by your friends and your teachers, it will have a greater tendency to become a fixed idea.

For example, if you believe that "honesty is the best policy", it's quite likely that somewhere in your background that idea became fixed in your subconscious mind through multiple sources of reinforcement.

Your parents may have told you, "Honesty is very important if you want to be a good person." A religious teacher may have told you, "God wants you to be honest."

In school a teacher may have explained to you that our society works best when everyone is honest. Perhaps being honest with your friends was highly valued in your social group. Perhaps you saw TV shows or read stories about all the problems that people experience when they are not honest.

Since the idea of honesty has been presented to you by so many different sources, it is quite likely that it has become a fixed idea in your subconscious mind. Now that honesty has become a fixed idea, if you do something dishonest, you experience a flow of energy that tells you that you have behaved in a way that runs counter to a fixed idea.

The energy that gives you that message is a feeling of GUILT! If you didn't have the fixed idea, then you wouldn't feel guilty when you violated it. Avoiding this feeling becomes a powerful motivator to abide by your fixed ideas.

From this we can see that society gives us many fixed ideas from multiple sources, which form common bonds and act as a unifying force in our world, although they may also cause conflict between social groups with different fixed ideas.

> **Key Principle 5: SIGNIFICANT EMOTIONAL LINK**
>
> **An idea is much more likely to be accepted at a subconscious level when it is linked to a significant emotional factor.**

Among some of the most common emotional factors are

1. Identification with a Person

You may have very loving feelings for a certain person. This can be used in programming if you are told that you are just like your mother or your father or your Uncle Charlie, and that you have the same problem they do. So, for instance, instead of someone just telling you that you're lazy, they present the idea to you as, "You're just like your Uncle Charlie! He was always a lazy bum. You're just as lazy as he was." The idea is always hurled at you in terms of weakness, but supposing you like Uncle Charlie and indeed prefer him to the person who's telling you you're lazy? Because of the positive feelings you have for Uncle Charlie, you're much more likely to accept the idea. The idea has been linked to an emotional identification that is a significant emotional factor for you.

2. Identification with a Family Trait

A mother says, "All the women in our family put on weight after they have a baby. My grandmother did, my mother did, and I did." What's the implication to the two little girls playing on the floor? "And you're going to do it, too, because you're female and it's a trait that all females in our family share". There are, of course, multiple factors in weight gain, some of them hereditary, but habits rooted in fixed ideas also play a major role.

3. Identification with an Ethnic Trait

How many times have you heard someone say, "I can't help it that I have such jealous rages. All Italians are that way." Or, "Sure I drink a little too much, but I'm Irish and it's in the genes." These are ideas that become fixed as a result of the person's identification with a supposed ethnic trait.

It All Comes Together

Now let's put all the principles together in one story and we'll see how one person can become, in their opinion, "The World's Most Disorganized Person".

Authority Figure

It's the second grade and one of the young students – Johnny - does not have the right shoes for the gym class. "Where are your shoes?" asks the teacher. Johnny's mind goes blank, he can't remember anything about his gym shoes, as he is called out in front of the others. "Aaah.." he says. "Why are you so disorganized?" asks the teacher, "Everyone else managed to bring their shoes to gym".

Emotionalized

Everyone in class laughs. Johnny doesn't realize that they laughed because it was a way for them to discharge their own tension, that it was just that they were glad that they weren't the one standing up in front of the class with their mind going blank. He feels that they are laughing at him because there is something wrong with him. There is a strong emotion present – embarrassment, humiliation. He feels that all the other kids in class have just confirmed that he is disorganized, through their laughter. *Everybody* knows he is disorganized.

Repetition

Now he has a self-limiting interpretation that says he is disorganized. A few days later, he is supposed to bring in something for "Show and Tell". Due to the limiting idea concerning organization, which is now operative in his mind, he forgets it is his turn and doesn't bring anything in. The teacher gives him a note for his parents, complaining of his disorganization.

Johnny brings the note home and hands it to his dad. Now, his dad has had to work hard and be ready for anything, all his life. So his dad is very concerned that his boy grows up to be capable and make a better life than he has had. His dad looks at the note and says, "What's wrong with you? Why can't you just remember what you need to bring?" This reinforces the limiting idea in three ways. First because the idea is being presented by another authority figure – his father, second because it's being presented by someone the child is emotionally linked to and who is showing a strong negative emotion in his criticism, and third because it's being presented through an additional source of reinforcement that is different from the classroom.

The father tells the boy, "You're going to get organized if it's the last thing you do. I want to see your class schedule every night, and you're going to tell me what you need to bring to each class, and put it right by the door. And I'm going to ask the teacher every morning when I drop you off at school, if you forgot anything the previous day."

Each time Johnny doesn't remember what he needs, and is asked by his father, "Why can't you get organized?" the idea is driven home with greater emotional impact and acquires greater power as a result of the repeated emotional reinforcement.

Multiple Sources

Now his older brother gets involved and says, "I don't know why you have so much trouble in getting organized. I never had any trouble being organized. Your sister never had any trouble, either. I don't know what's wrong with you." Now, we've seen multiple reinforcement taking place, from a variety of sources. We've seen it emotionalized and repeated by authority figures. Now we'll add the final step.

Significant Emotional Link

One day his mother, who's upset by all of this that's been going on with Johnny, takes him aside and gives him a hug. Then in a confidential tone of voice she says, "Don't be too concerned about all of this, dear. You're just like me. I never could get organized, either!" His mother has just added an emotional identification! A person Johnny cares for has the same problem, and the process of fixing the idea is complete.

Thirty years later, this person may come to me and say, "I am the world's most disorganized person. I'd forget my own head if it wasn't fixed on, and I've always been that way." Now you can see how that idea became so fixed in the subconscious mind. The irony is that the idea that he is fated to be disorganized is a delusion. There are genetic influences on traits such as dexterity and analytical thinking, which make it easier for some people to learn to be organized than others.

But if the same amount of energy that went into creating and reinforcing his idea that he is disorganized, had instead been put into the project of accepting that he started out with a certain basis for organization, and teaching him how to improve it, he would be in a very different position.

Chapter 13

READINESS FOR CHANGE: TWO STEPS, THREE TURNING POINTS

STEP 1: DISINVESTING FROM RESENTMENT

It is tempting to look back and say, "When I think of how my father, who was so brutal, beat me up all the time, and how my mother, who was always so sarcastic, never gave me any approval, it's no wonder I'm the mess that I am today." This applies, of course, not only to parents but to any other figures who were significant in the creation and reinforcement of our limiting fixed ideas.

I must caution you at this point. You need that energy that you have invested in resentment, to transform it for creative use in your life today. It cannot be in two contrary investments at once. So liberating it, by giving up all the energy that you have invested in that kind of resentment, is the first step in committing to change. That means that if you now recognize that your behavior is contaminated by fixed ideas acquired in childhood that other people played a role in creating, your road to liberation is to stop blaming those people and come to a hard, even painful, realization.

> No matter who created the problem, YOU are the only one who can or will deal with it, for no one else can or will. YOU are the only one who can or will find the ways, the means, the methods to change those ideas and feelings within yourself. Whatever roles others played in your past, are now yours to play.

STEP 2: INVESTING IN THE PRESENT & FUTURE

A rule of physics is that you can't create energy, nor can you destroy it. It can only be transformed. Most children have obvious energy. At that early stage we have little awareness of the resistance the external environment may put up to our plans. We have what has been called the most precious gift of the mind, a belief in ourselves.

However, most of the people I have seen in my therapy work are intensely critical of themselves. If you are wondering whether this applies to you, if your answer to the question, *"Who in all the world would you treat as meanly as you treat yourself?"* is "no-one", then that early belief in yourself that made the day hopeful and glorious has now been transformed into beliefs that make your days miserable. So our task is to **reverse that movement of energy**, and to do that, we need to understand how energy is moved by the way we think.

Pain & Pleasure

The subconscious mind has two major movements. The first is the movement away from pain. This is the strongest movement, because it's linked to the survival mechanism. The second is the movement toward pleasure.

Often we see people staying with mental, physical or emotional pain and we say that they have developed a conditioned tolerance to pain, which is called psychic masochism. Masochism overrules the natural tendency to move away from pain. It is literally amazing the degree of endurance that some people will display, suffering from problems that they don't need to have.

Psychic masochism develops as a result of earlier experiences that we interpreted in certain ways that generated certain feelings, usually feelings of low self-worth. Those feelings led to certain thoughts, such as that we cannot expect much except pain, it's all we deserve, and those thoughts led to certain forms of behavior, such as tolerating pain and disrespect, expressed in specific situations, such as in relations with others, or our goals for our lives.

Readiness for Change

The philosopher William James said that all human beings resist change until they reach a point of readiness for change. How do we overcome that powerful resistance and become motivated to change? To my knowledge, there are three major ways.

Motivation 1: I've Suffered Enough

Suffering can be mental, physical or emotional.

Physical suffering always has a mental and emotional aspect. Sometimes this aspect may be crucial to causing the physical suffering, as in stress-related or psychosomatic conditions. Sometimes, our mental anxieties and emotional distress may add to the physical suffering we have. My belief is that there is almost no physical condition where the patient cannot benefit from the input of creative imagination. This can be to reduce suffering from physical symptoms such as pain, to gain mental relief from the distress caused by their symptoms, to enhance energy for recovery, or to gain mental cooperation with treatments that may be hard to endure.

Mental suffering consists of constantly expecting the worst in the area of your problems. Very often, our critical faculty can tell us that our thoughts are irrational, and we find ourselves arguing within ourselves, with our own thoughts. Clients who come to see me will characterize themselves as stupid, because of the "dumb" things they're thinking, yet they are smart enough to know that what they are thinking is dumb! Establishing a hypnotic contract with ourselves through self-hypnosis, can be the start of listening to our own intelligence.

Emotional suffering, sometimes also called psychic suffering, is inevitable in human life. When we lose a loved one, or something we enjoyed or were attached to comes to an end, for instance, we suffer. In an emotionally healthy person, we then go on to recover and find enjoyment in life again. But there are some people who don't enjoy life nearly as much as they could, not because of any particularly bad events that happen to them, but because their emotional habits are out of control.

The Turning Point

You can reach a point of readiness for change because you've suffered enough. Change can take place when the kind of modifications that you've had to make in your lifestyle because of your problem – your adaption, in other words – become painful enough for you that you then become ready for change. We say, "I've had enough. I've suffered enough." Sometimes this can happen all at once, in a moment of major revelation, other times, a person has become embedded in many layers of suffering, it can take a series of turning points for them to free themselves from pain. They succeed in overcoming a small, present problem, and then progress to unraveling the whole knot that is tying them down, step by step.

Motivation 2: Psychic Boredom

The second element that can lead to readiness for change is what I call psychic boredom, that is, a lack of meaning in life. All of us need to feel that we have something we can center ourselves on, something that gives our life a sense of meaning and purpose. This will naturally evolve during our lifetime, as our understanding develops through experience, but our sense of what is important and valuable is needed whatever age we are.

The problem is that at some point in our lives, many of us close down that very important imaginative faculty that we can use to reassure ourselves that somewhere in the world – maybe even somewhere over the rainbow – are the people, the circumstances and the situations that will one day come together to help us fill our deepest needs.

What are those needs? Well, we start with attempting to fulfill our basic physical needs. Those include the needs for food, shelter and clothing. After that there are needs for acceptance, affection, love and approval. When we get those needs reasonably satisfied, we can then move on to the next level, which is our need **to actualize our potential and to be all that we can be**.

However, as we go through life, unless we use a powerful counteraction such as self-hypnosis, there is a natural tendency to shut down that imaginative faculty that we use to keep our hope and expectancy alive that we will succeed in expressing our uniqueness in the world. We can feel ground down and defeated, and give up. And once that faculty is closed down, we begin to approach a state called **despair**. Despair is a product of hopelessness – in fact, the word despair means "without hope".

The Turning Point

When we close down our faculty of hope, a terrible existential despair strikes, which creates terror in us. At that moment of terror, as you approach the borderline of hopelessness, you are faced with two possible responses.

One possibility is that you can become life-negating. That means entering into anti-life behavior. That means suicide, which can be quick – through any of a hundred ways the imagination can conceive to bring about rapid death. Or it can be a slow form of suicide – through addictions to alcohol, drugs, food, compulsive sexuality and other kinds of enslavement.

The second possibility is that as you approach that borderline of hopelessness and you become very desperate and very anxious, you can face your need for change. Then you can reach out for help in an effort to become **life-affirming**. You've reached a turning point.

Motivation 3: Realization that change is possible

The third factor that can lead us to a point of readiness for change is when we become aware that change is possible for us. A student said to me, "I'm at a place, in a moment of my existence when that disbelief about myself begins to dissipate. It's like that morning fog that rolls in over the coast from the ocean, and as it begins to burn off you see holes in that fog. I begin to see a hole in the fog of my unbelief, and at this point in time, I begin to suspect that I can change." Needless to say, I was very happy to hear this.

The realization that change is possible – for YOU – can be brought about by a book, a sermon, a class, a friend who changed, and many other sources. However, **an external inspiration can only ever be a trigger for something that comes from deep within yourself.**

A true turning point requires staying power. To be effective, the realization that change is possible has to acknowledge the sometimes harsh realities of life. There are many superficially appealing but insufficient and misguided philosophies on offer. For instance, sometimes people hold to the very appealing idea that if you think the "right" thoughts, evil vanishes. However, this on its own may often be an insufficient defense. Evil exists in the form of harmful intentions of people, and their actions that have consequences and effects. These effects can be mitigated and dissipated, but this takes realism and effort on our part.

The question arises, how far can you be led by the message of others, until your own creative intelligence speaks to you? You're the only one who realistically knows what's satisfying, rewarding and fulfilling for you, because for adults there are no authority figures. Only children require parents, and only children need authority figures. Simply to blindly follow the dictates of others, however amazing, unusual or different their philosophies may be – unless it leads you back to your own problem solving mechanism and your own decision to take responsibility for your life in this moment and forever more – is to accept a false message.

You must be self-directed. You must realize that there are teachers and there are communicators, but there are no people who can direct your life correctly for you.

And when you reach the turning point?

I can't predict whether you're at that place of readiness for change. No one can, not even you. Only you will know when you get there. Reaching a point of readiness for change can take decades, but changing direction inside yourself from hopeless to hopeful, is a choice which takes place at a particular instant, in an instant. Cynical disbelief is a form of conditioned helplessness. Then suddenly you reach a point at which you say, "Maybe this is the day, maybe this is the moment, the person, the book, the sermon, the time, the hypnotist that can really move me to know, to believe, to develop a conviction that *I too can change!*"

My teaching is ready here for you, when you're ready. It's the best thing for me to hear, in my work, when a person says something that amounts to, "I think I'm finally coming to a position from which I can believe that it's possible for me to change."

If you're using self-hypnosis, do you have to discover your subconscious limiting fixed ideas and work against them? It can be an appropriate route for a person to enter a therapeutic process as part of liberating themselves from deeply fixed ideas that are opposing their attempts at self-change. If this is available for you and you find it helpful, good. There will be occasions when the original fixed ideas have been so powerfully installed and reinforced over the years that it is appropriate to seek the help of a professional therapist. As a therapist myself, I often work with clients in this way and it can be very helpful to speed up the movement toward change.

But in many cases, you've outgrown the cause. The cause might have been your emotional reaction to the fear of abandonment – to the fear of rejection by a parent. But that was part of your experience back then and is just a memory. It's just a memory that you keep active by continually playing it back like a player on a stage. You become an actor on a stage who only knows one role – one set of lines – and when the curtain goes up you play out the same old role and speak the same old lines.

Changing roles, changing scripts

When we look at life in dramatic terms, we play a great variety of roles, and we learn many lines. We have many ways of acting and reacting in a great variety of situations. Sometimes when a person feels locked into a role you hear them say, "Well, that's just me. That's the way I am." These limited adaptions are restrictions they have placed upon themselves. What they fail to see is the great flexibility that's part of each of us.

We can play many changing roles. It's part of a healthy adaption to life to increase our range as we learn from our experiences. We can say, "in this situation this is the role that I can play. I can just do it quite easily to increase communication and relationship, and as a human being, I am fully capable of doing that."

Choosing goals that are right for you

Your goals will develop as you achieve them one by one. Your first goal may be to lose some weight, or to get started in a career, or to enjoy social events. Accomplishing any goal gets you to a new position, where you can have a more expanded goal. The goals you have further along in time, you could not conceptualize when you started, because you have expanded in vision and effectiveness with every goal accomplished.

As we start on this great work, as you gain the power to achieve your goals, it's important to learn to set goals that are true and healthy for you. I want to clarify something about the concept of self-improvement and to understand a very important fact about ourselves.

> **Any self-improvement plan based on rejection of parts of yourself is not healthy for you.**

But what you can do is to begin to integrate those parts of yourself that you despise instead of trying to amputate them. The moment you stop trying to push them away, you suddenly gain control of them. When you gain control, you can manage them and soon they disappear as negative behavior patterns and their energy is transformed for you to use as you choose.

I want you to **take the word "should" out** of your goals. You see, "should" is what "isn't", and you must deal with what "is" - your actual self. Don't give yourself any "shoulds".

The Truth about You

Don't say, when you're developing a program and choosing words to put in it, "Oh, they're beautiful words and phrases, but not the truth about me, so if I say it, I won't really accept it."

You cannot measure programming in terms of true or false. If you wanted to drive a screw into the wall and you went to the tool cabinet and you picked out a hand drill, you wouldn't say, "Is the drill true or false?" You ask, "Is this the tool I need to get this job done?" So ask yourself, **"When I am successful in internalizing these ideas into my subconscious mind, will they produce the result that I want?" If the answer is "Yes", then they are indeed the truth about you.** For ideas can only stimulate and motivate you to action.

> **The truth about you is that your potential is infinite in nature.**

You can only dimly perceive it at any given time, but it continues to expand infinitely as you move toward it. When does your potential end? Think of all the great people in history. Did their influence upon the world and upon the universe end because they died? Our ability to program energy out into the world is infinite in nature, just as our potential is infinite.

The process we are engaged in is **de-hypnotizing** you first, so you can surrender your adherence to the delusions that you have accepted about yourself. We are participants in the ascent of mankind. Our individual effort is part of that ascent. We cannot refuse to move toward our potential, because in doing so we attempt to betray ourselves, and everyone who went before us.

When we see ourselves in this perspective, we feel a greater sense of responsibility about our need to be all that we can be. By this

I mean that your life becomes creative, expressing your unique, ascending character and desires.

I'm going to give you one idea that will help you to understand your relationship to your potential, which is infinite in nature. Hold on to this idea.

> "I acquire all the knowledge and all of the skill and all of the tools that I need in order to realize my fullest potential and to actualize my deepest nature and to fill all of my deepest needs as I continue my movement toward it."

Now the key word there is "movement". You have got to move toward your potential. You've got to be taking some kind of action.

And for that, to overcome the old ideas that limit and obstruct you, and replace them with new, transforming ideas, you need effective programming.

So the next step is learning how to do that.

Conceptualization
Visualization
Emotionalization
Actualization

1. Be Positive
2. Use the Present Tense
3. Be Specific
4. Be Detailed
5. Be Simple
6. Use Exciting & Emotional Words
7. Affirm Activity
8. Be Accurate
9. Be Realistic
10. Personalize

Chapter 14

PROGRAMMING – FOUR STAGES, TEN RULES

The Four Stages of Programming are

> Conceptualization
> -> Visualization
> -> Emotionalization
> -> Actualization

Entering the state of hypnosis is usually easy, with a little practice. What takes more thought, is knowing how to correctly structure the suggestions that you give yourself in the self-hypnotic state. Most people have it in reverse, they think, "If I could only learn to hypnotize myself, the rest is easy."

It's very important how you structure your program. People think, "Programming I can do because it's my mind and my problem and I know how to talk to my mind." But your current situation has been created, at least in part, by how you have been talking to your mind. So this needs to change.

The fact is that if you don't follow the proper rules, your own suggestions not only won't create the proper result, but they may even deepen the very problem that you're trying to overcome. This is why we have studied the Rules of the Mind about how ideas are accepted by the mind. So now we learn how to use these rules, to program ourselves effectively.

Conceptualization -> Visualization

In programming, chains or series of related ideas come together to form concepts. When those concepts acquire sufficient intensity, they begin to flash up spontaneously as imagery. It's not enough just to tell yourself, "Oh, just visualize that. Imagine yourself." It is the series of related ideas forming concepts, that process of conceptualization, that causes the visualization to flash up.

Visualization -> Emotionalization

You can't begin to get the appropriate feeling until you can first get the appropriate image - "I can see it and now I can begin to feel it and get excited about it" - which leads to taking action.

Emotionalization -> Actualization

Because you can't get out there and do it until you feel like doing it. And when you feel like doing it, what was difficult for you to do before is now becoming easy for you to do, to actualize.

> **Programming Rule 1: Be Positive**

Words are signals that ring bells. "No", "not," and "don't" are all neutral words as far as your subconscious is concerned, they don't ring bells, or produce images. But the words that you put next to these "no" words, do create images. It's that simple. People who have never had training in how to structure suggestions make this mistake all the time. They continually talk about what they want to move away from, and that only reinforces the problem.

Example: A shy, self-conscious person is giving themselves a "pep" talk before going to a party, so they tell themselves, "When

I go to that party, I'm not going to be nervous and self-conscious. I'm not going to be afraid." Which words have the greatest emotional energy? "Nervous" and "afraid". Instead, they need to develop positive, creative ideas that will create an image or a scene of what they want, such as, "I like people. I enjoy meeting new people. As I arrive at the party tonight, and as I walk through the door, there's an expectant smile on my lips; a twinkle in my eye." This creates, very simply but very powerfully, the kind of situation that this person is interested in experiencing. We're not painting a picture of the experience they don't want.

Don't talk about what you want to move away from; talk about what you want to move towards. Don't talk about what you want to remove from your life; talk about what you want to bring into your life.

Programming Rule 2: Use the Present Tense

The subconscious mind is an **existential mind**, which means it's only in "the moment". It's true that you can remember the past, and it's true that you can imagine the future. But it is only in this present moment that you can experience your response to the memory of the past or to the imagining of the future. That's what we have to deal with – your emotional response in the moment.

To use the present tense means that we create a picture of it happening now – this instant.

You see, most of us are always planning on getting it all together in the future. It's a form of expectation that is really just idle daydreaming. When you fail to use the present tense, even your best expectations simply become intentions that will never become actualized. **When constructing your suggestions, you specify when they are to take effect and you describe specific behavior.**

Example: Supposing you have to give a performance or a presentation on October 19th. Here's how you structure suggestions for that. "On October 19th, as I step on to the podium, I am calm and poised and relaxed. I speak easily. I deliver my lines fluently. My actions are perfectly tuned and timed." And so on. Notice that I'm speaking in the present tense even though I'm referring to future behavior that will occur at a very specific time.

You must be careful to **avoid the past**, as well. When you talk about the past, you are reminding yourself of behavior that you wish to change.

Example: If you say, "From now on, I'm not going to have violent temper explosions toward my children every time I get upset," then again, you're being negative. You're reminding yourself of what you want to move away from. Instead, talk about what you're going to do. "I speak with love and understanding to my children, and they in turn feel good toward me."

Sometimes you must use a variation of the present tense, known as the **"progressive form" of the present tense**.

Example: If you had a broken leg and you had it in a cast, if you said, "My leg is strong and well and perfect," there's a part of your mind that says, "Then why are you wearing the cast?" Instead, say "Each day the healing powers of my creative intelligence are healing, strengthening, and making my left leg more powerful than ever before. Each day my leg is stronger. This accelerated, rapid healing is occurring in me right now."

Programming Rule 3: Be Specific

To be specific means, don't say things like, "Every day in every way, I'm getting better and better." That doesn't create any specific images of any kind. It's too vague and too general. To be specific means to isolate a single area that you wish to work on. Then begin to create your programming in that area. You notice that in the programming script for confidence in a previous chapter, all of it was about specific actions and elements relating to those actions. There were no generalities in there.

Select and focus on a single area until you see some result. That could be in a day, it might be in a month. If you've worked with a program for thirty days and you're not getting any measurable results, or in other words, if you can't measure it and no one else has said, "Hey, I see you're changing and I like it!" then review and revise your script, with some expert guidance if you feel this is required. You may not have developed an appropriate program or it may be written incorrectly, or you may be focusing in the wrong area, your subconscious energy is not engaging with the topic, or the way in which you're approaching the topic.

When time pressure applies: suppose you have a number of things you want to work on. How do you decide which one to start with? Suppose one of the things you want to work on is situational. You're preparing for an exam. It's coming up in the near future and you've got to deal with it right now. Then based upon the fact that you have some time pressure about getting ready, in your self-hypnosis you would work only on preparing for the examination. After that's out of the way, then you would begin to deal with something else.

When time pressure does not apply: when you're not pressured to deal with something situational, here's how you make your selection of what to work on when you have a number of different goals. You begin by looking at these goals that you've set for yourself and you say, "What's the most important one in my life right now?" Then you give it a priority. You go down the list in that way and number them one, two, three, four, and so on.

But here's the surprise. Don't start out with number one. Instead, go down the list and let your first programming be on five or six or seven. You see, in the beginning **you must think of this inner power that you're taking control of as a newborn infant. It's going to grow very rapidly and become very powerful, but in the beginning, it's got to be nurtured.** So you don't want to start using it in a very important goal in which there's likely to be a lot of subconscious energy invested. You want to get a couple of successes first. Because that will rapidly expand your confidence in your ability to use your own energy on your behalf.

Programming Rule 4: Be Detailed

Don't use generalities, that is, don't try to structure your suggestion like a bumper sticker and say, "I am always enthusiastic." You're always going to be enthusiastic? Clearly, there are many occasions, such as a funeral for instance, when enthusiasm is inappropriate. To be detailed means to **isolate every element of the problem and program suggestions in that area.**

Here's how you can do this. You already know what you dread or dislike about something, so isolate all the negative elements. For instance, if you fear public speaking, you can list, "I'm afraid of people. I'm especially afraid of people when I stand up to speak to an audience. As I begin to speak, my mouth feels dry, my lips feel stiff.." You carry on listing everything negative about the experience. The elements of this problem are now isolated in a negative way. Then you take each sentence and you flip it over using the positive antonym and it comes out as, "I like people. I enjoy speaking to people. I especially enjoy talking to an audience. As I begin speaking I feel a wave of friendship and understanding flowing from every member of the audience to me and I in turn feel friendly to them. I want to do things for them. As I begin speaking, my lips are flexible, my mouth is moist.."

I took all the negative suggestions and I turned each one over and found a positive antonym. That's the way you develop a program. It could apply to singing or dancing as well as speaking. It can apply to any performance about which you have a feeling of shyness or reluctance.

Programming Rule 5: Be Simple

Speak to your subconscious as if it were an intelligent nine-year-old child. Avoid "literary expression", this is not an academic exercise written for a teacher to grade. Avoid technical words or phrases, and complicated sentence structures. Look again at the script on Confidence – it consists of a **flow of simple statements, short straightforward sentences that form concepts, that lead to visualizations.**

Programming Rule 6: Use Exciting & Emotional Words

Be sure to use words that generate enthusiasm and response from your subconscious – your subconscious is your feeling mind. Learn to use words such as Vibrant, Sparkling, Thrilling, Wonderful, Powerful, Radiant, Loving, Generous, Abundant, Exciting, Delightful, Beautiful, Joyous.

Programming Rule 7: Affirm Activity

Describe actions, not abilities, in your suggestions. For instance, don't say, "I can do ...", or "I have the ability to.." This does not create a visualization of action. Say, "I do..", "I am..".

Programming Rule 8: Be Accurate

Don't aim for the stars with the intention of hitting the top of the mountain. You don't need to overshoot, to state excessive goals in the hope of moderate results. Your subconscious is not fooled – it is part of you and knows that you're tricking it. **Be straightforward** and open about your true goals in your programming.

Programming Rule 9: Be Realistic

This essentially means **avoiding perfectionism**, often this is expressed by the use of "always". Don't say, "I am always on time and organized." This is setting yourself up for failure and self-criticism. Select wording which allows for human error and fluctuation, such as "I organize my time well and make good preparations for important things."

Programming Rule 10: Personalize

Remember that you cannot change others directly, so don't structure your suggestions to suggest change in others, always personalize them to yourself. So, don't say, "My friends appreciate and respect my efforts to entertain them." Do say, "I like to entertain people. I enjoy organizing events and having guests over." Often, when your attitude and behavior changes, others respond positively.

Putting it All Together

Look over the script on Confidence, and see how you can check off these programming rules, which have been used to structure that script. This gives you ideas for how you can create your own effective programming.

And in the next and final chapter, we're going to put together what you've learned, so that you are fully capable of creating a powerful program of your own.

Chapter 15

NINE STEPS TO HYPNOTIZING & PROGRAMMING YOURSELF

We're now going to learn the principles of hypnotizing yourself in combination with the programming that you've developed for yourself.

Recording and Live Options

You have the choice, when self-hypnotizing and self-programming, to record yourself and listen to the recording, or to program yourself in your mind. We'll discuss some issues relating to this later. However, it may not always be possible, or convenient, to record a program for yourself when you want to use one, or you may be without your recording equipment in some situation. So in this chapter we're going to learn how you program yourself in your own mind, and I strongly recommend that you learn this invaluable, self-reliant method.

Here are the nine steps to take to develop these skills:

1. Write out your Program

Until you've written it out, you don't really have any idea what you want – all you have is a collection of hazy and nebulous ideas that come into your mind and then leave again and are a bit different the next time. The moment you begin to write out your program, you begin **crystalizing the concepts that relate to your goal.**

In this first step, you write down your programming, then you edit it, revise it, expand it, condense it, and keep checking it against the ten Rules for Effective Programming I gave you in the previous chapter, to see whether or not you are following all of those rules for greatest effectiveness in your program.

After a while, you'll come to a place where you're satisfied with your program. You'll develop the feeling, **"If I can get these ideas accepted at a subconscious level they will become the basis for my new behavior, then I know that I will truly change."**

2. Create a Symbol

A symbol is a word or a phrase that by implication stands for all of the content of your program. For example, suppose you had a couple of pages of programming designed to increase your self-confidence. The symbol might be something as ordinary as, "Dynamic Self-Confidence." You use the symbol in this way. You write at the beginning of your suggestion, "Dynamic Self-Confidence is the symbol for the following ideas." Then you begin your programming. It's even better if you personalize your symbol, using something unique and personal to you, rather than just adopting an abstract kind of a phrase.

Example: A man was having trouble losing weight until he came up with a symbol that worked for him. The symbol he selected was "Army Uniform." He came up with that symbol when he had been cleaning out a closet and he came across his old army uniform. He said, "I slipped on the coat, and it was then I realized how big I had become since those army days. I could remember what great shape I was in then and how I was able to go through that obstacle course. So I just decided that was my symbol. Every time I use that symbol, 'Army Uniform', all of those ideas and feelings well up from somewhere inside me and automatically I'm pulling in my stomach, I'm straightening up my shoulders, I'm standing erect." He said, "I use it especially at mealtime, and I find that I'm eating less."

You see what a symbol can do for you. You can create your own symbol. **That symbol goes at the beginning and it goes at the end** of your program.

Now you've written your program, you've developed your symbol, and now you need to get ready to hypnotize yourself.

3. Establish a Suitable Place

You establish a place where you're going to practice. It might be the bedroom or the den. Once you've decided where you're going to do it, that this is now your practice place, your next decision should be to **make sure that the environment is appropriate**. Suppose you've chosen the bedroom, but on the other side of the bedroom wall is a television set or computer game machine. And other family members are using this, and you can hear it through the wall. You know that you can doze off with the television on, but when you go into a trance, your hearing is more sensitive. The sounds – perhaps theme music, shouting, or action sounds – are going to start triggering thoughts that will interfere with your hypnosis and programming.

Now you have two options. Either you get a set of earplugs or noise-cancelling headphones or you say to the family, "I'm going in to hypnotize myself, and I'm going to be about thirty minutes. So you're going to have to turn the sound down low." Working parents, in particular, often have great difficulty in reserving time for themselves. They say, "Well, I'll wait until I get the kids in bed and the dishes cleared," and so on. And then, of course, they have the excuse that they're too tired and they'll do it tomorrow. **Change starts when excuses stop.** Parent or not, your goals are important, and being a parent who can use self-hypnosis and programming to direct and change your life is one of the best inspirations and role models you can give to your children.

Don't attempt to hypnotize yourself in a room where there's an air conditioner or a current of air blowing across you. Your skin's surface becomes very sensitive when you're in a trance, and cold air sensations will inhibit your letting go. It's better to be a little too warm than to be too cool. You may want to have a blanket and just pull it up over you. As your body relaxes, your veins and arteries relax as well, and your blood pressure automatically drops. That means that your body temperature may drop a half a degree or a degree. Some of you who are very sensitive to that will feel cold. Check out these things and make adjustments. It may take a little experimentation for you to find just the right set of circumstances to maximize your response.

If the room you're going to lie down in is near to the kitchen, or other source of smells, keep in mind that you become used to the cooking smells after you've been exposed to them for a while and you no longer consciously notice them. If you've been cooking fish or something that has filled the air with cooking smells, even though you aren't consciously aware of them, your subconscious will continue responding to those odors when you're in trance. It might give you thoughts of food, and it might stimulate your appetite. If that's the case, use a deodorizing spray in the room before you go in to do your self-hypnosis, or make sure the room is thoroughly aired with fresh air, or both.

4. Set a Time of Day for Practice

Another thing is to test the time of day to find which is the best time for you to hypnotize yourself. Some good times to hypnotize yourself when you're starting out, are about an hour after your evening meal. Don't wait until you get into your bed at night. If you always hypnotize yourself at bedtime, you'll develop the habit of relaxing and then going to sleep. Then at another time later on, when you're sufficiently practiced at self-hypnosis to be able to do it at any time, you'll hypnotize yourself at three o'clock in the afternoon and you'll respond to that habit of falling asleep. Unless you suffer from insomnia, don't use bedtime for the purposes of self-programming.

For the same reason, instead of lying on the bed, you might want to take a pillow and lie down on the floor. Your mind doesn't associate lying on the floor with going to sleep, unless you're one who sleeps on the floor, in which case, lie on the bed to do your self-hypnosis!

Later you might discover, as many do, that to awaken a half hour early in the morning and use that time for self-hypnosis and programming is very effective, to set the tone for the day.

5. Read your Program aloud.

The next step is to read the program aloud. Do not read it silently because in reading silently we are accustomed to scanning and skipping. When you have properly developed your program, every word is significant. You want to read it aloud.

You read it aloud because you're using a number of avenues to your subconscious mind. When you read it you are using the faculty of sight. When you speak it aloud, that's a second avenue, and as you speak it aloud, you hear it, and that's a third avenue. This is **preprogramming**, building expectancy that is then realized in the trance.

6. Get into Position and Start your Trance

Now you've read the program aloud. Next you stretch out into a comfortable position. The best position is on your back, or if you can't do that, sit in a comfortable easy chair, or the most comfortable seat that you can. Now do exactly as you've done when listening in the practice we've done earlier.

You fix your eyes on a spot on the walls or on the ceiling. Stare at that spot for about fifteen seconds just to eliminate all visual distractions. You take three deep breaths. Each time you exhale, you say mentally, "Sleep now." Why do you say those words? Those are the words that are in the earlier scripts. Those are the words that you've become conditioned to. If you try saying, "Now Sleep", it won't work as well. If you say any other combination of phrases, it won't work as well for you because you're not conditioned to those words. On or before the third time you exhale and say the words, "Sleep now," let your eyelids close down.

Now don't be concerned about whether they want to close on the first time, just let them close on the first breath or the second breath or the third breath. Some people say, "I have difficulty holding them open until the third breath." Don't let that affect you. Close your eyelids down whenever you wish to. First, second, or third breath.

Now just as soon as your eyelids close down, you'll begin to feel that wave of relaxation in the same way that you felt it while listening to the recorded or read aloud script before. Why? Because you've been internalizing this script and your subconscious knows,

"I'm here to do this, just as I was here to do this while I listened before," and it will begin to play back in your mind.

Many students have reported that they hear the voice speaking just as it did on the recording. This means that you just took the voice from the recording and transferred it into the recording database in your mind. It's like having a playlist of your favorite songs – all you have to do is focus for an instant, and it works in the same way.

7. Preprogram how long you will be hypnotized

The next thing that you do is to picture an analog clock, with a circular dial and hands pointing to the figures. This clock is very large, and the hands are set for ten minutes from the time that you start this self-hypnosis process. In the beginning you make it for ten minutes. Later you can do it for longer periods of time. Then you mentally give yourself the following suggestion. "In exactly ten minutes from now, my eyelids open automatically, I'm calm, rested, refreshed, relaxed, and I feel good." See the hands of that clock. Look at your watch as you lie down. If it's now seven o'clock, in your imagination see those hands set at ten past seven.

You can, of course, set an alarm or a timer for a few minutes later, as a back-up, but just as you are learning to do without a recording if you have to or want to, so you are also learning to do without a timer if you have to or want to, and develop your own, "in-house" programming.

Don't try to calculate the passage of time while you're in hypnosis. Don't say to yourself, "It must be three minutes or six minutes or eight minutes." Students report that the subconscious mind tells them it's time to terminate the trance in a variety of ways.

Some say, "My eyes just suddenly popped open," or, "I just became aware that it was time to open my eyes." Some say they hear a little alarm going off, usually the sound of an alarm they actually use in their daily life, say, to waken them in the morning. When you finish your session and "wake up", look at your actual watch or clock. Check the time. It often is within a minute or two of the ten minutes that you've set for yourself.

If you don't immediately find that your subconscious responds to your timing preprogramming, set your back-up alarm and persist. You will learn a lot about your relationship to time from how you respond.

After you've successfully done ten minutes three or four times, move it to twenty. After twenty, move it to thirty and forty until you can put yourself into a trance and tell yourself that you're going to lie there an hour, if you want to, and automatically terminate it. You can do it as so many others have. I've taught more than twenty thousand people to use these principles effectively.

8. Think your Symbol.

The next step is to think your symbol. You think that word or phrase that is linked to the programming that you read a few minutes earlier. The key here is to take it easy, don't try to punch it home. Just think it mentally once, twice, three times. Then let your mind drift where it will. Don't try to remember the wording of the suggestions, but let your mind just float wherever it will.

9. Let the Subconscious Mind run your Program

Now let your subconscious mind run through the program. You lie back and enjoy the relaxation, until the program reaches the termination that you wrote, and you return to your full awareness once again, at the end of the time you set.

Alternate termination of trance

Now rather than have the subconscious mind just terminate the trance at the end of the preprogrammed time, there is another way. However, it involves you being focused enough to do it, and often students report to me that they drift off once they start, and then their subconscious terminates the trance. So the alternate is, if you're aware enough, you can simply say, "I'm going to count to five. At the count of five my eyes are open and I'm fully aware and I feel good." Just as it says in the script, then count yourself up. Be sure to use those same good, positive, powerful, creative suggestions which are designed to bring you out of trance with a feeling of well-being.

Persistence overcomes resistance

Don't be concerned if initially you feel a little negative response from your suggestions. That's the old forces fighting back. But you're going to overcome them. You're the general and you have a mighty army and you know the power of your forces to overcome the evil of negative thinking and feeling. Negative feedback is informative, and the information tells us how we have to strategize to work past the fixed ideas that are resisting.

Let me give you an example of someone I worked with, who experienced just this kind of resistance when she started self-programming. She came to me with the realization that she was on her own, instead of in a relationship as she wished, because she always found something wrong with every relationship partner. She had recently come to understand that objectively, many of them would in fact have been good partners, but she had found fault, and pushed them away. We worked on an affirmation for her, and came up with, "I accept myself as a lovable person. I easily express love and approval. I eagerly accept the love and affection that surrounds me now." I recommended that she repeat this several times throughout her program.

She reported back to me that as she tried to say, "I accept myself as a lovable person," her throat closed, she couldn't get the words out, her heart began pounding and she broke out into a sweat. She had then changed the words to, "I accept myself as a likeable person," and she managed to say that. This showed us where the problem was! She pushed potential relationship partners away, always finding some excuse, so they would not find out that she was unlovable. She persisted, and was able to expand her goals and accept that she was lovable. She was then able to make a happy and successful marriage.

Symbolic Associations

Now as you continue to work in this manner, you'll find that when you say your symbol, whole phrases will flash up automatically from your suggestion script. You're getting the true action of autosuggestion. After a while you'll find that you automatically begin to think of your key words consciously, not just in the programming session but while you're carrying out your everyday tasks, and words and images will begin to flow up. Now, you've really got it working for you.

You can attach a little signal to the symbol, that can be used consciously, not just in the programming session, when you want to call up the feelings that you've been programming. Let's say that your programming has something to do with taking an examination. I suggest to my students that they do something like cross the first two fingers, take a deep breath, and mentally say a few words as a key phrase. For an examination, the words might be, "Calm, poised and perfect recall," and you do this as you begin the examination. This acts as a trigger to release all of those programming ideas and affirmations from where they have been stored in the subconscious mind.

The Finished Product

The process of combining your programming into your self-hypnosis is really very simple. I have taken it apart element by element so that you can see it and assemble it just like you put a jigsaw puzzle together. Now you look at the whole picture, the finished product, and you say, **"That was really easy, and I can see it clearly now."**

Making your own Recordings

If you make your own recordings, there are a few aspects that you need to consider.

Let's talk first about the "person". People say, "Should I address my subconscious mind in the first person and say, 'I', or should I address it in the second person and say, 'you'?" Personally, I address my subconscious mind as "you". If you're concerned about this, then you might use both and run an experiment. First give the suggestion in the first person, and then repeat it in the second person. Then listen to it and see how you respond best.

The next point is, how well do you respond to your own voice? As opposed to, how well do you respond to a hypnotherapist's voice on a recording? In the beginning, you may not have very much belief in yourself and in your ability to direct your own energy. So sometimes you have to be weaned away from recordings made by a hypnotherapist, and make your own recording that you then play at alternate sessions. In that way, you begin to get a blending of the energy. Slowly you build confidence in your response to yourself and to your own voice. So that at a later time when you may need to, you are able to program yourself and accept your own self-programming at a subconscious level, because you trust yourself.

Developing a relationship with your subconscious - Creativity and Problem-solving

We can't all be champions in athletics or in every public situation, but we *can* be champions within our own milieu. We can be an inspiring role model for the people we are close to and for our associates.

Your options may be restricted in various ways, but you can go ahead and do what you can do. You can develop the mental expectancy that will enable you to become a champion in whatever you endeavor to be and to accomplish.

All that I have taught you here is entirely natural – it arises out of discoveries about the nature of the subconscious mind. I've talked to many creative and successful people who have told me, when I describe self-programming, that they habitually do this anyway, and have done so for years, without ever knowing that there is a science of self-programming, and teachings in the subject! They worked it out themselves, through naturally developing a relationship of integration and inner harmony between their conscious and subconscious minds.

For example, one student, whose work was to invent medical devices, told me that when he got stuck working on an invention, he would lie down to go to sleep at night, and say to his subconscious mind, which he called "Old Charlie" – "All right, Old Charlie, I'm turning it over to you." He kept a pad of paper right by his bedside, and he used a pen that had a little light inside that lit up when you wrote, so that when he woke up with ideas in the middle of the night, he could write them down. He said, "Many times when I look at the pad of paper in the morning, I find a drawing or a formula and I don't even remember waking up to write it down, but it's there." And many other students have told me of similar experiences, whether related to work problems, or personal problems.

These examples demonstrate that the subconscious does have creative, problem-solving power, and in order to draw on this, you first have to be open to receiving from it, that is, you must trust it. You must turn the problem over to it. You must believe that deep source of power and wisdom and energy is within you. It's not just transcendental, up in the clouds somewhere. It is transcendental *and* right here with you, and concerned with everything you do. From the start of developing your relationship with your subconscious, doing the suggestibility tests, through your regular practice of self-hypnosis, you are working towards a fuller and fuller opening-up of the resources of your inner world.

That energy that animates the universe flows through you in a very special way that enables you to be a creative being. Isn't it exciting just to think about it?

Trance and Meditation

Many people study philosophies and systems that recommend the practice of contemplation and meditation, often for similar purposes of inner harmony and inner development as I am teaching here. Many of these systems have their roots in places where members of religious orders would dedicate their lives to achieving the required states of mind, in particular, the ability to "clear" the mind from all thoughts.

This is often hard to do, especially if you don't live in a monastery, and people therefore can give up or achieve very limited results. This is where knowledge of self-hypnosis can be very helpful.

There is no inherent conflict between meditation and hypnosis. The human mind is the same, being used for both. The idea that you are not fully in control of your own mind during hypnosis is a misconception, as we have seen. And hypnosis can be used to clear the mind. The difference is that using hypnosis usually makes this much easier.

Here is an example of an exercise which can give you practice in clearing your mind of thoughts. As usual, you can read it aloud and record it yourself, get someone else to read it or record it for you, or use a recording of mine.

Read aloud/Play recording:

Preparation: Sit back comfortably in an easy chair or other comfortable arrangement. Place your two feet flat upon the floor. Fix your eyes up at a spot up on the wall or on the ceiling.

Induction: Take a deep breath now. Exhale. Sleep now.
Now a second and even deeper breath. Exhale. Sleep now.
Now a third deep breath. Exhale. Sleep now.
Eyelids close down.

Visualization: I want you now to imagine that you are standing in front of a house. This is an unusual house. It's twelve feet high, twelve feet wide, thirty-six feet long. There are three rooms, one behind the other. And this structure stands over a basement. There are three steps that lead up to the house.

I want you to walk up and open the front door. As you do, you step into the first room. It's a very unusual room because there is only one piece of furniture in the room, a reclining chair. The carpeting, the walls, the ceiling and the upholstery on the chair are all a beautiful sunny yellow. This is called the Yellow Room. The chair looks so inviting that you walk over to it, sit down in it, and push it back *into a reclining position. You feel so pleased, and as you do, you let your mind drift to a pleasant experience of the past thirty days. A pleasant experience of the past thirty days. [15-second pause] And now the memory causes you to feel even more relaxed.*

But it's time to get up from the chair and move on to the next room. Now you are getting up from the chair, and you move to the second doorway and step inside. This room is almost identical to the first, except the color is gold. This is the Gold Room, and there is that reclining chair in the center of the room. Since your experience was so good the first time, you walk to that reclining chair again, sit down in it, and now you just lean back. As you do, you bring into your mind the memory of a very pleasant experience of the past twelve months – the past year. [15-second pause]

Alright, it's time to get up from that chair, and you move into the third room. This is the Blue Room. It's exactly like the first two, except for the color. You walk to that chair, you sit down in it, and you lean back. But as you lean back, there's something very interesting occurring. What's occurring is that the chair now is on a hydraulic hoist, and it begins to slowly move down. It's going down into that lower level, passing right down through the floor. As you're going right down, deeper, sitting in a very relaxed, comfortable position, now it stops and you're down into the basement.

Now as you stand up from the chair, there's one door ahead with a sign that says, "The Room of Nothingness". You walk to the door, turn the knob, and step inside. As you do, your eyes narrow down and you hesitate, because it's very dim in this room as the door closes behind you. There's a strange feeling beneath your feet, because you're standing on a foam rubber pad which is three inches thick.

Now the door is closed and your eyes slowly become accustomed to the gloom. There is a kind of rosy glow in the room. You take a few more steps in and you decide to just sit down. Now you sit down and you feel this soft foam, three inches thick, cradling you so comfortably that you just decide to lie back. Now all the light is gone and the room is filled with nothingness. And as you lie there, that nothingness moves across your mind. You mind is filled with nothingness. [5-second pause]

<u>Termination:</u> *I'll count from one to five. At the count of five, eyelids open, fully aware, feeling wonderfully good.*
One. Slowly, calmly, easily and gently returning to your full awareness once again.
Two. Each muscle and nerve in your body is loose and limp and relaxed. You feel good.
Three. From head to toe you're feeling perfect in every way.
On number four, your eyes begin to feel sparkling clear.
On the next number now, eyelids open, fully aware, feeling wonderfully good.
Number five. Eyelids open now, take a deep breath, fill up your lungs, and stretch.

Did you recognize the mental misdirection induction? While your attention was distracted by creating the visualization, you entered trance and the suggestion of mental nothingness was accepted. You can amend this visualization if you wish, if there are images you would prefer, and remember the rules of effective programming – this "nothingness" script follows them all, check it out!

CONCLUSION

If you were a student in one of my classes and we had reached this point, we would be saying goodbye. But a reader is different. This book, and myself as I speak through it, can stay with you.

I hope you read and re-read it many times, that it, and what it teaches, are with you on your journey through life and that through it, and what it teaches, you come to understand and live the beautiful truth about yourself.

Check out our website
westwoodpublishingco.com

for other works by
Gil Boyne
including programming recordings on

Dynamic Public Speaking
Weight Control
Stop Smoking
Self-discovery
and many others

Also audio and printed works by
classic masters in hypnosis including
Dave Elman
Ormond McGill

and other training materials